She Speaks

THE INTIMATE MEMOIRS OF....

Chinaza M. Duson

Leslie,
From a yatcht!
To helping others!
Change this lives!
Let's tell the story!

—Chinaza

www.fast-print.net/store.php

COPYRIGHT © 2003-2015 and written
by Chinaza Marali Duson

She Speaks Global LLC
c/o Chinaza M Duson
phone: 404.464.6733
email: shespeaksglobal@gmail.com
website: www.shespeaksworldwide.com

Cover Photographs: Reggie Anderson Photography
Cover design & text layout: David Springer

First published 2015 by
FASTPRINT PUBLISHING
Peterborough, England.

An environmentally friendly book printed and bound in England by
www.printondemand-worldwide.com

This book is made entirely of chain-of-custody materials

Mixed Sources
Product group from well-managed
forests, and other controlled sources
www.fsc.org Cert no. TT-COC-002641
© 1996 Forest Stewardship Council
FSC

PEFC Certified
This product is
from sustainably
managed forests
and controlled
sources
www.pefc.org
PEFC/16-33-415

"We are hard pressed on every side,
yet not crushed; we are perplexed but not in despair;
Persecuted but not forsaken; Struck down but not destroyed;
For we who live are always delivered to death for Jesus sake;
Therefore we do not lose heart, for our fight afflictions
which is but for a moment, is working for us a far
more exceeding and eternal weight of glory."
~ Corinthians 4: 8-13; 14-17 NKJV

Dedication

*This book is dedicated to those who
I've yet to meet. For my children, Indira & LJ, for
reminding me of why I am here. To my beloved Grandfather,
Carlos Duson, thank you for protecting me, never forsaking me
and for being the angel assigned to me in each appointed
season. Thank you, Anita, for the memories, the storms,
and test you subjected me to. For they've made me
resilient, God fearing, and proud to be his child.*

Contents

Prologue

January 12, 2008

I had been living in Atlanta for nearly eighteen months and was gravely homesick. I wanted so badly to return to California, but my finances prohibited an immediate move. I was bored with the monotony that Atlanta's Metropolitan terrain presented. My social life was null, and more often than not, I found myself socializing alone. On one particular evening, I visited Atlantic Station, Atlanta's premier hot spot, which was located in Midtown. My journey to independence was a slow stroll, but it took a complete stranger (who shall remain nameless) that I encountered to ask the questions I was deliberately trying to avoid—*"What hides behind those baby brown eyes that I can't see? Who stole your confidence?"*

Although I am a self-professed "ball of expression," it has been difficult for me to describe the pain that has been somewhat of an immovable, yet driving force within me for many years. Unlike the 10 calamities that besieged the children of Israel in Egypt, each with a different message and lasting a finite period of time, my personal plagues have lasted for more than 30 years. Somehow, I grew immune to them, and my internal suffering became more intense with the onset of each new episode.

In retrospect, I realize that God put me through storms symbolic of the rivers of blood, flocks of frogs, flies, unbearable boils, hail mixed with fire, locusts, seasons of darkness, and the death of my first born. Truthfully, all of the storms in their own unique way have affected my "land"—life. If I went deep into my history, I'd find the symbolism of what God has been trying to unveil to me to, which had been buried deep within for the last 38 years. In the end, I know that I am more than this compilation of stories. In short, these experiences are to birth something else out of me.

Two weeks after that brief meeting with the stranger at Atlantic Station, my eyes were suddenly opened to a self-perpetuated reality that had theretofore been blinding me: Self! I began to question myself, wondering if it really had been 30-plus years of searching that brought me to that pivotal moment—throughout all the relentless selling of my soul for pennies on the dollar, the bumps and bruises, the contusions to my psyche, the emotional destruction of my own pathway—before I was finally able to stand up and demand that the real me, as well as the soul within me, return to its origin. So, I thus call all that I am about to share with you "a few lessons learned."

August 12, 2007

It had been three years since I penned the first draft of this memoir. I initially entitled the manuscript, *Defying the Odds*. Can you believe it? I actually thought my purpose was fulfilled, or at least that it come in phases. When I completed Phase One of this nearly 80,000-word testimonial, I assumed I would have hit the literary circuit by now and that the world would have been forever changed. Interestingly enough, however, that wasn't what God had in mind. In the first draft, I hadn't truly broken my silence. "I" was my own worst enemy, holding myself back. But I learned that God's timing doesn't line up with ours. In essence, He had very different plans for me. He let me know that there was still so much for me to tell, and He reminded of how His word declares, "We are overcome by the power of our testimony," not half-truths, not selectiveness, but by our "testimony." I discovered just how selfish I was when I omitted so many key things in the first draft of the memoir. I was sent back to the drawing board. This time, not only had God sent me back to *Defying The Odds,* but he also gave me a new title—*She Speaks*—An Awakening of a Revolutionary Voice!

God birthed the title in my spirit shortly after I met 'George Tisdale who I later wrote about and branded an "Innovator of Urban Retro Rock". We met on the social networking site MYSPACE in 2006, and amazing enough, what the world may have referred to as a "coincidence," was merely one of many divine appointments predestined by God for us to fulfill our purpose. When George called me in the summer of 2007, needing a place to crash, my doors were open. We became like brother and sister, and he moved to Atlanta with a mission to let the world know through his music know that they, too, were "Born Free."

One afternoon, George informed me that he and his business manager decided to emulate the business model of another artist whose project had been broken into phases. With that, he and I collaborated to define the phases of the Born Free Movement. In an instant, four words were penned on a piece of paper—Liberation, Independence, Faith, and Emancipation.

It was in this moment that God revealed to me that just as George's music spoke truth and gave life to its audience, I had to write my story in total transparency. It was revealed to me that when I finished writing my story, it would liberate every audience that read it, give independence to those who were confined in their minds, bodies and spirits, emancipate the millions of souls living in silence, and utilize faith to direct persons to their divine purpose. After all, it was about Him. It was then that my purpose became clear; I would tell my story so that others could be free. I would stand up and speak loudly. Jesus' life was the perfect example. His life was symbolic because he went to Calvary so that the world could live, and in turn, he died and paid an ultimate price for our freedom. This meant that I to was "BORN FREE". This inspiration drove me to brand myself with those very words. I would later get them tattooed on my shoulder. In an instant, my purpose was clear, my heart was full, and I began to write.

My initial omissions in *Defying the Odds* stemmed from my fear of what others would think. Although born Tiffany, my name is now "Chinaza," meaning, "God answers." And to those of you who will read this testimony, I pray your life is forever changed. For there are nations waiting for you to show up so that others may know that God's word never returns void nor is He any shorter than His word. Men and women of God, I tell you that He does answer prayer! So open your mouth, inhale from the bowels of your belly, and begin to pray. You hold within you the key to your destiny; within the locked doors of your soul, there is purpose, power, and more importantly, the Holy Spirit! Reclaim your independence and celebrate God's wondrous works!

As you read this memoir, you might discover things that relate to your life. I ask that you allow God to guide your heart and your footsteps toward your own Independence Day, and be not afraid to tell the truth as to how you became free. Seek God's "best wine" first so that He will bless you beyond what your eyes and ears can ever see or imagine! The journey begins in your mind, for the mind is the enemy's battleground! You cannot place new wine in old wine skins; it just won't work. I dare you to dream bigger! Dream bigger faster, think bigger than yourself; plan bigger plans than your peripheral can see, look beyond the blue skies—for God has no limit! It is my prayer that all over the world God will release His spirit through these pages, enabling every yoke to be broken and destroyed. Forget about your failures and dysfunctional past; they will become a distant memory as you pursue your purpose and live your destiny out. I am living proof that it's never too late to become what you should have been and to start all over again. Take a journey with me so that you, the chosen one, can launch your Independence Day! I forewarn you, however, that the process is neither glitzy nor glamorous. It is God's way of getting you right where He needs you! Look at it this way, God's grace has led you thus far, so don't ever stop moving forward! Your Destiny belongs to you. Get it, get it!

Let's go back in time to Chocolate City, a.k.a, Washington, D.C., on March 7, 2003— a parenthetical place marker in my life. Dinner that evening was at one of my favorite spots on the border of Capitol Hill, The Caucus Room, a veritable 'Who's Who' of politics and business dining located in the Congressional District. My dear friend, Vashion, and associates, Steve B., India, and Tammy, accompanied me on this go-around. I had regularly eaten in this restaurant's darker corner during my many sporadic visits to the City. On this evening, however, I was greeted with many "I miss yous," high energy, hearty handshakes, bear hugs, and kisses.

We kicked off the evening by ordering a liberating truth serum, a 2000 bottle of Longoria, Pinot Noir, and a Bruschetta appetizer. As everyone placed their orders, we all raised our glasses and toasted to placing the weekly grind behind us. As the evening progressed, our idle chatter grew louder until it resembled the screams at a Lakers game; I couldn't hear, let alone think sensibly. When the appetizers arrived, I began sharing the details about my latest failed relationships and nonproductive business ventures. With a sly chuckle, Steve interjected with a barrage of disparaging questions—

"Charlie Brown, when's the doggone movie coming out, girl? 'Cause none of us can keep up with you. You're 'As The World Turns,' and 'One Life To Live,' - a mini-reality series! Are you ever going to settle down long enough for life to catch up with you? You're moving non-stop. I only wish I had the energy and time to live a life as 'interesting and busy' as yours. Where do you find the time? And, by the way, how are the kids?"

His questions threw me for a loop, literally stunned me. I couldn't respond. I didn't know how to! "Charlie Brown' was one of the many nicknames given to me due to my fast-talking, New York accent and the physical size of my head. I must admit, Steve's statement bore some validity. My life appeared to be a never-ending soap opera. I was always determined to get "somewhere," at any cost. After the life I'd lived, stopping to laugh and smell the Frappuccino's from time to time wasn't optional, it was a necessity. I thought I was living the life— I worked in a highly political career field that gave me increased professional and visible notoriety, especially after the attacks of 9/11. But it, in return, made my life more hectic. I had no balance. I was a 26-year-old professional who was at the top of her game. At the same time, I was a single mother whose children were suffering the absence of a mom, due to my absence. Bear in mind that I vowed never to allow anyone to walk in my shoes without vigilantly trying to help them, especially my children. But deep down I knew that everything that glittered wasn't gold. While I had walked many miles within the last twenty-six years of my life, I knew that I had much to get done if I were going to please God the way He demanded. Hence, I became driven by getting "things" accomplished in my life, no matter the cost.

However, as I was accustomed to doing, even when I felt uneasy, I smiled graciously and simply responded, "Thank you, baby. When I find out, I will let you know. In the meantime, let's take this thing one day at a time! I'm determined to write a book and take my voice to Oprah's doorstep."

Vashon, a staunch supporter interjected, "Aww, man, don't sleep on Chi because everything this girl said she would do, she has done. So, if Chi's saying it, you can trust it's going to happen. Chi, just tell Oprah I said, 'Hello,' and don't forget us little people when you make it big."

It was an uplifting compliment, but I had to wonder whether I had truly done everything I professed to doing. Honestly, I hadn't. I was riding high on a fantasy, and telling the truth about the "real me" was too scary. Besides, it made me more mysterious, or so, I thought. I found myself in a season where I was too consumed with the opinions of others, still bound by my past. As a matter of fact, I had to ask myself, *What is my purpose?* Truthfully, I hadn't trusted God enough to reveal it or provide me with the provision to carry myself to it. I just thought I knew how to handle my own. Not. I had heard countless times how driven and determined I was, but, I wasn't convinced. You see, the words "You'll never be anything" had more power than "awesome," "smart," "bright," "articulate," and "beautiful." I revisited these words often and spent a great deal of my years trying to make what someone said about me "not amounting to anything" a complete fallacy. I had mastered the art of an external disguise. On the flip side, I remembered others tell me how much potential I had; that I had so much purpose. I, however, wasn't clear. It wasn't that I couldn't hear God for myself—I had simply chosen not to. In my heart, I wanted others to know that I was more than an average Jane in a good suit with a compilation of short stories—I was called and destined for the nations.

In order for others to believe it, though, I had to first. Vashon's comments brought on yet another ah-ha moment for me. I knew that it was time I got over myself, time I ventured beyond my own veil and accepted the reason I existed in the first place. It required me to dig deep. It was time for me to become driven about something other than my circumstances, my vanity, my wardrobe, my career, and more so, being plain ole stuck on myself. It was time I sought out this same God Who created and knew all about me to unveil my purpose, and, in doing so, He said it again, louder and clearer, "TELL THE STORY, WRITE THE VISION, and MAKE IT PLAIN."

∞ ∞ ∞ ∞

Fast forward with me to Tuesday, February 24, 2004, which was almost a year later. I was in Oakland, CA. I decided to attend a women's meeting at Greater Saint Paul Full Gospel Baptist Church. As always, the meeting began in prayer, and I only knew how to pray for God's continuing grace and guidance over my life and heart. I prayed the prayers of what I heard others say. Why? Well, I didn't quite know how to pray, so I took the traditional approach, which was simply saying what I'd heard others say. Again, I didn't truly know God for myself. I only knew that I had been given an assignment, a vision, and that I was on the hunt for provision. A young woman, who we'll call 'Bethany,' stood up and introduced herself on behalf of the Evangelism Committee. I assumed she was an evangelist (how else could she be speaking on their behalf?), not to mention that her dress reminded me of my days in the Church of God in Christ where the women wore dresses down to their ankles. While she looked a little outdated and bland with no makeup, her voice rang with a level of excitement unlike anything I had ever heard. Loudly, she blurted out, "Ladies, it's time we told OUR story! It's time for us to tell others how God brought us out, so that they, too, can live!" The words uttered from her lips sounded eerie, as if God were saying to me again (for the third time), "WRITE, TELL YOUR STORY." It was further confirmation of what I had heard in my spirit!

Her words rested heavy in my spirit, and my spirit was on fire! I wanted to leap to my feet, shout, praise Him, clap my hands, cosign on her sentiment. But instead, I sat still, selfishly silent and observant. I was more consumed with what others' impressions of me were. Yet I knew that there was a time bomb ticking inside of me. I had just received some more great news, another confirmation, which I could only smile about because God was still speaking to me, even in my disobedience. On this night I actually heard Him and opted to do something about it! I've learned that to hear God, one must be still. The greatest challenge is whether we are truly listening.

∞ ∞ ∞ ∞

CHAPTER ONE

In the Beginning

In the beginning, there was Adam and Eve. Now, when you examine the dichotomy in the bible, here is a picturesque family that was infused with blame and ended cursed in tragedy. When Adam consumed fruit from the forbidden tree and was banished from Eden, he blamed Eve for having first eaten of the fruit and subsequently causing him destruction. We can assume that their bickering probably continued for many years and was most likely, a bad example for their children, Cain and Abel. This dysfunctional family then became worse when Cain became jealous of his brother, Abel, and murdered him. My point is that so many families today are burdened with generational curses because of the actions of someone else. Freedom is about casting down labels and curses. As with the biblical "First Family," oftentimes, someone is blamed for the things that go wrong in our family members' lives. So who do you or your family blame for the things went wrong in your life? With that being said, allow me to introduce you to the beginning of my life.

My grandmother, Anita Roberts, was born on August 8, 1924, in Arlington, Georgia, a small town in Duval County whose population was barely fifteen hundred. She grew up smack dab in the middle of the Great Depression, a time when many folks participated in tenant farming, producing crops of cotton, tobacco, peanuts, and grain, in an effort to support their families. Unfortunately, many families, instead suffered from extreme poverty. In effort to establish a better life for my grandmother and her siblings, my great grandparents packed up and moved from the South and into the northeastern part of New York.

The family settled in Buffalo, New York in the late 1930s, right at the time when a large number of African Americans were moving to cities and urban areas to work in the war industry. This "Great Migration" initially seemed like a liberating movement, but instead, it resulted in a great period of suffering for the African American community, overall. My grandmother's family, along with most transplanted African American families, moved into the Lower East Side of the city, joining a small, but thriving black community. They took up residence at 251 Cedar Street, the location where they remained for two years before relocating to Adams Street.

Blacks quickly filled the emptying vacuum, and, as their community grew, it strengthened. The surrounding white world, however, was hostile. Segregation was accepted in every branch of the city's social, economic, and political sectors. To ensure that they received a good education, my grandmother's parents put her and her siblings in Catholic school, where they learned how to read and write, eventually leading them to being labeled as extremely bright children.

At age fifteen, my grandmother dropped out of school to help support her family. She took a job at Westinghouse. During this time, which was in the early 1940s, Westinghouse was involved in the military-electronics industry, and, thanks to World War II, business was booming. Job security looked promising, and my grandmother was proudly and very successfully contributing to the support of her family. It was during this time that my grandmother met her first husband, Robert Taylor. He would go on to father her oldest children, a set of twins who, sadly, who were stillborn. The experience left my grandmother emotionally devastated. However, she had no time to coddle her emotions. With a family that still needed the economic support from her income, she continued working at Westinghouse.

In 1942, my grandmother gave birth to her eldest daughter, Gail, ultimately marrying Gail's father, John Clinton, after divorcing her first husband, Robert. Her marriage to John was short lived, ending four only years later when John left my grandmother alone and pregnant with their second child. Despite the break-up of her marriage, she rebounded and began courting a young man by the name of Madison Bridges, all while still carrying her second child by John, her daughter, Patricia.

My grandmother and Madison's romance started out beautifully but quickly turned sour. Anita discovered very early on in the relationship that Madison was abusive. Unable to live with him because of the ongoing abuse, this marriage, too, came to an abrupt end. Unlike the previous marriages, by the end of her marriage to Madison, my grandmother's once sweet spirit was broken. The effects of Madison's abuse left her with a bitter resentment of men. In fact, she had seemingly grown to hate them, evidenced her emotional tailspin that caused her to lash out, both verbally and physically, at anyone in her way.

Two years would pass before my grandmother met Carlos Duson, a sweet-talking, charming Texan with Creole roots by way of Texarkana. Carlos had also migrated to Buffalo in search of a grand employment opportunity. But not long after he arrived, he discovered that he wasn't quite cut out for a 9-to-5, ultimately taking up gambling as a profession. He became a prominent no-nonsense "bookie," hustling black market numbers. He landed huge profits that allowed him to provide well for his family. Having vowed to never to remarry, my grandmother took a chance on Carlos and began dating him.

He romanced her and loved her deeply. He believed that he could mend her emotional wounds, but my grandmother's reasons for staying with Carlos were purely financial. She kept the promise she'd made to herself and did not marry Carlos. Nevertheless, Carlos moved his newly-adopted family to 31 Welker Street. The two-bedroom home was extremely small for their growing family. In June of 1955, my grandmother gave birth to a set of fraternal twins, Conitra and Dennis. Two years later, Denise, her last child, was born.

In 1963, at the age of thirty-nine, my grandmother was caught up in the sweeping layoffs at Westinghouse. Rather than return to the workforce, she opted to become a housewife and stayed home with her five children. The money she collected from her pension and SSI benefits (due to her diabetes) barely supported the family, so she sought employment once again. She could no longer rely on the gambling money from Carlos, because it was inconsistent.

Finding it virtually impossible to land a job, my grandmother began to lose hope, causing her fragile mind to become a repository of negative thoughts. She reflected heavily on the overwhelming amount of adversity she'd dealt with in her lifetime—her multiple failed marriages, the deaths of her children, the separation from her parents, and the stress over the loss of her job at the hands of what she believed was the 'white man's doing'. Most of her disappointment turned to anger, and she used Carlos as a dartboard for her pain.

"If I could, I would leave you and all of these damn children," she'd threaten on multiple occasions.

But believing she could change, Carlos, who I would affectionately call Granddad, stayed, partly for my grandmother's well-being but mostly for his children's well-being. In doing so he witnessed my grandmother slip into a manic-depressive state, using habits such as smoking, gambling, and drinking to numb her pain. Her feeling of dependence on a man became unbearable. After all, she was the same woman who had prided herself on her ability to stand on her own two feet and provide for her family. She didn't like handouts; she believed they came with a price. Her staunch belief that the white man owed her led to a never-ending 'blame game' facade. Having watched her family rise up from slavery, Anita harbored bitter resolve and believed her ill will was everyone else's fault. She became increasingly erratic, and it wasn't long before the angry woman with no transferable skills, no high school diploma, and who was no longer the breadwinner of the family finally snapped, morphing into a physically abusing maniac.

By the end of 1963, my grandmother's eldest daughter, my Aunt Gail, left home. The years preceding her decision to leave had been brutal, having suffered repeated episodes of physical and emotional abuse at the hands of my grandmother. For reasons that Gail never understood, my grandmother would often beat, starve, and isolate her oldest child, Gail. Finally, when she couldn't take anymore, Gail decided to leave home. However, what Gail initially thought would be her great escape turned out to be the worst decision of her life—she met and became quickly romantically involved with Charles Gibson, a smooth city-slicker. She lived mainly on the streets, allowing her new lifestyle to suck her into its enticing and corrupt ways. Her deep depression over the eventual abuse caused her to make one bad decision after another—she had three children in three years and was unable to adequately care for any of them. In 1966, after the weight of a bad relationship and a childhood riddled with nightmares finally proved to be too much for Gail. She overdosed on aspirin and alcohol, leaving her three young children, Theresa, Marie, and Antoine, without a mother. Charles, their father, was nowhere to be found when Gail died, even now, his whereabouts are still a mystery. Since my grandmother was her only known relative, my grandmother, by default, was left to take custody of her grandchildren.

Theresa, Marie, and Antoine were much too young to mourn their mother's death, and my grandmother had no room in her hardened heart to do so either. She deeply resented having to take care of her grandchildren, and shortly thereafter, began physically abusing Antoine, Gail's middle child. And Antoine would go on to be repeatedly sexually abused by a close relative.

No one ever really delved into the real reasons behind my grandmother's abusive behavior toward her own children and grandchildren, although some family members hypothesized it might have been some type of psychological response to the traumatic events in her own life. There were even some identifiable patterns associated with her abusive behavior. Nonetheless, she managed to never harm a hair on the head of Gail's baby daughter, Marie, or her own baby daughter, Denise, proclaiming that they were "God's gifts." The other children in my grandmother's care, however, received no such favorable treatment and therefore suffered immensely, both physically and psychologically.

After sometime, Carlos, her then boyfriend, began to notice scars on Antoine's body. Confronting my grandmother about it, only made matters worse. In her rage, she once grabbed a pair of scissors and stabbed Carlos in the chest and leg.

"That'll teach ya ass to stop asking me questions!" she screamed, slamming the bedroom door behind her. She was vicious and dangerous when she was angry.

Not wanting to incite her rage any deeper, Carlos acquiesced. He loved my grandmother, but more than that, he feared her, so he kept quiet, especially after she pulled the same scissors that she had stabbed him with and chased him through the house. No one knows whether Anita really felt any remorse for what she had done to Carlos. But the fact that she brought him a concoction to place on his wound and helped him cover the wound with a bandage served as a symbolic gesture that perhaps she did, because from that day forward, she never physically attacked Carlos. She did, however, abuse him with words, more often than not.

Conitra, my life's centerpiece, was a dark-skinned, longhaired, striking beauty. Her beautiful smile was said to be the irritant that started my grandmother, Grandma Anita, in on beating her, although no one knew for sure. Also, for reasons unknown, my mother was silently dubbed the black sheep of the Duson family. My grandmother went to extremes when it came to punishing my mother, beating her with books and extension cords and often locking her in the basement of their Welker Street home. There, she would spend days at a time, sleeping on the concrete floor under the stairwell in the middle of winter, miraculously enduring Buffalo's brutal winter nights. During extended bouts of abuse, she went without food and water and was forced to stew in her own excrement.

When she didn't have my mother confined to the basement, my grandmother had her either sleeping with the dogs or locked in the closet. Many times, she even made her eat her meals in the closet. That is, when my mother was allowed to eat. The only explanation that my grandmother ever offered for treating my mother this way was simply, "I hate her," she'd say. Although Dennis wasn't subject to the same horrific conditions as my mother, he wasn't totally immune. He had his share of whippings at my grandmother's hands.

A fateful event that occurred one night during the summer of 1972, would cause my mother's life to never be the same. My grandmother sent my mother to the corner store to fetch her a pack of cigarettes and some snacks. Perhaps she was intuitive, or maybe she was just being stubborn, but whatever the case, my mother did not want to go. She complained to her niece, Theresa, during the entire walk to the corner store.

"I think it's ridiculous for us to be walking out here this time of night," my mother vented.

"You know we have no choice," Theresa answered. She wasn't in the mood to debate about what they should or should not have to do. She knew they really didn't have a choice. She also knew that my mother would be held responsible if they didn't get the items they were sent to the store for in the first place.

"Go find the Ginger Ale," my mother instructed as they walked into the store.

"You go get it yourself," Theresa said with an attitude before storming off.

"Hey, Theresa, get back here," my mother yelled.

But it was no use. The corner store door slammed behind Theresa, and she disappeared into the night on her way back home, leaving my mother to carry the entire bags home by herself.

"That'll be seven dollars and twelve cents," Mr. Jennings, the corner store owner said, looking over his glasses at my mother.

My mother pulled the crumpled dollars from her pocket and handed them to Mr. Jennings.

"Thank you, darling," Mr. Jennings said, taking the crumpled dollar bills from my mother.

Barely making eye contact, my mother mumbled, "You're welcome."

After engaging in some small talk with Mr. Jennings, while he bagged her groceries, my mother then took the bag of groceries and headed out of the store into the dark night. Darkness was all she could see and feel—darkness in the road ahead of her and darkness in the road behind her, both literally and figuratively. She continued to walk, nonetheless, with the sound of her soaking wet shoes hitting the pavement reminding her of earlier days when she would walk home from school in the rain as an adolescent.

A noise behind my mother startled her, and without looking back, she picked up her pace. *If I can just make it to the streetlight up the road,* she thought. She heard the noise again. This time, it seemed a little louder, it was closer. When she turned around, a big, burly black man stood before her. From her estimation, he looked to be about six feet tall, but she couldn't make out the intricate facial features. She could tell, however, that he had big, round piercing eyes. The hairs on her neck stood up. Instinctively, she dropped the bag of groceries.

Before she could utter a word, the man grabbed my mother by her hair and pulled her close to him. "What are you doing out this time of night, huh?" he said, not at all interested in her response. He was merely insinuating that she shouldn't have been out that time of night, giving him unrestricted permission to violate her.

Before my mother could reply, he placed his left hand over her mouth. "You gon' get what you came out here for," he said, swinging my mother around and pressing his manhood against her buttocks. "Get down on the ground," he instructed, unzipping his pants.

Having been no stranger to physical abuse, my mother acquiesced and did as she was told. She had no fight in her. She was a mere ninety-eight pounds and was certainly no match for the six foot, two-hundred pound-er. The violent thrust of his manhood in and out, in and out...made my mother's entire body, including her sens-es, go numb. The pain between her legs ceased, and she could no longer hear sounds of cars driving by or the sounds of the crickets lying underneath her. She couldn't even see the big, round face of her attacker—only sheer darkness.

When he was finished doing his do, he rose up and straddled himself over my mother. "You see, this...is what...hap...happens...to fast-tail girls that come out this time of night," he said, panting between words while simultaneously tucking his manhood back into his pants. "Now, I'm gon' make sure you don't back go running yo' mouth," he said added, retrieving a box cutter from his back pocket.

Now able to see the blurry shadow of the big, burly man straddled over her, my mother's eyes shifted to the image of the box cutter he was holding up. However, she never flinched. Perhaps she felt death was her rescuer, in that instant. Life for her had certainly been no bowl of cherries. If it has to end here, so be it, she thought.

Without further hesitation, her attacker slid the blade of the box cutter across my mother's neck. Blood oozed from the wound. Everything went black, and a lifeless Conitra lay battered on the bacteria-ridden concrete.

With a minimal amount of strength, she managed to roll over and drag herself out of the alley. She climbed the stairs of a stranger's home, cried out, and then passed out. When the homeowner came to the door and discovered my mother lying there unconscious, she immediately dialed 911. My mother was rushed to the hospital, where doctors fought diligently to repair her slashed throat.

While the average person would have marveled at the miraculous sparing of my mother's life, my grandmother's heart remained as cold as Buffalo's record-breaking temperatures. She showed no emotion and never even comforted my mother after learning of the tragedy.

"She got what she deserved," Anita said, callously. "If she was out there showing her ass, then I'm glad someone got her ass!"

One would think that such a tragic event would have sparked some compassion and love in my grandmother toward my mother—but not so. My grandmother had a heart full of hatred and was clearly insensitive to the fact that her own daughter had been victimized. When my mother returned home from the hospital, my grandmother immediately jumped on her.

"You out there telling people that sh*t was my fault cause I sent you to the store?" she said, banging my mother's head against the woodwork in the hallway.

Weak from the rape, my mother fell down on the floor.

"Get the hell up! Get up! If those nosy azz people come knocking on my door, I'mma knock the hell outta you again!" my grandmother threatened, kicking my mother for added emphasis.

Brutal beatings and abuse were nothing new to my mother, but she obviously endured one too many. She eventually left home with the intention on never returning. She was taken in by her aunt, Patricia, who hoped she could save her little sister. Little did she know, however, Patricia's good intentions would not help as much as she had hoped. Her niece had been locked up for the last ten years and had recently cheated death. Now, with a 'get out of jail free' card in her hand, my mother had no clue on how to react to her newly discovered freedom. The move seemingly solved one problem for my mother but did nothing to answer the million-and-one questions running through her mind—*What do I do now? To whom do I turn? Where do I go from here?*

At age 14 and with no one to guide her, my mother followed her older sister's path and soon became addicted to the streets. Her aunt, Patricia, had a work schedule that didn't afford her an opportunity to maintain much order or control, so my mother came and went as she pleased. And it wasn't long before my mother took to the corners of Main Street and Utica. Patricia tried the best she could to rein her sister in by taking off work to be hands-on with my mother, but the attention associated with the street corner was more exciting than anything my mother had ever received at home. She didn't know what it felt like not to look at the insides of dark closets or not being confined in basements for days at a time. She instantly became hooked to the people and the fallacy of what the streets offered. Within months of moving in with her aunt Patricia, my mother reconnected with her younger siblings, Denise, and her twin brother, Dennis. They introduced her to Dennis's friend, Johnny, a well-known pimp who, along with Dennis, pimped women up and down Utica and Chippewa streets.

"If you want to make that money and do good, you gon' have to work the streets hard," Johnny would often remind my mother.

"What if I want to quit?" my mother asked, looking forward to the day when she would find a better way out of her circumstances.

Johnny laughed. "You don't quit the streets; they're too addicting. It's a way of life for people like us."

My mother must've taken Johnny at his word, because for the next four plus years, she ran the streets with Denise and her newfound crew. The lifestyle she lived was perilous, but she couldn't seem to leave it alone, not even after she witnessed Denise getting stabbed.

∞ ∞ ∞ ∞

After escaping abuse and cheating death, my mother certainly should have been enjoying life, cherishing the fact that she was still around to live it. Instead, she had nothing and no one and was forced to use the treasure between her thighs to support herself. She was among the ranks of the streetwalkers in Buffalo's "Red Light District," which ran from Chippewa street all the way through the "Fruit Belt," one of the poorest neighborhoods in the city. It wasn't a life that anyone in their right mind would have chosen, but my mother wasn't in a position to make choices—she was merely surviving.

Even after seeing how mean and cold the streets were, my mother wasn't convinced that she was in any more danger than the danger she'd faced at home. When her father begged her to come home, she agreed. But her stay was short-lived, because my grandmother didn't want her around and the abuse resumed. My mother left home again, this time, for good.

Not long thereafter, my mother dropped out of high school. To her, "freedom" meant running back to her pimp, Bernard, who was quick to put her back out on the streets. Prostitution took her far from reality and somehow calmed her frustration of being poor. She believed the fast life was better than anything she had experienced. After enduring numerous years of brutal neglect, emotional, physical and sexual abuse combined with growing up in an environment devoid of love from her mother and siblings, she was left seeking other avenues to fill the void of emotional neediness. Dennis, my mother's twin brother, was supposed to look out for her, but he became too consumed with recruiting more women into prostitution to boost his income.

The streets were all my mother had, and since she had vowed never to return to 31 Welker Street, she was willing to live the street life for as long as she had to, just to survive.

She would never forget the words my grandmother barked when she left home for the last and final time.

"Good, stay yo ole' ass out there! Don't nobody want you no way."

"No Safe Harbor..."

She sees the shore
Through all the wind and rain, she sees
destination but must travel through pain.
The current is not kind, but carries her
where she longs to not go.
The briny taste of seawater seems to be
the only thing that she knows
But she rows onward hoping to find
a cove.
A place of rest where her anchor can
be dropped
She is tired of treading water
continuously being stopped.
There is no safe harbor that she can find
No beacon of light to guide her home.
She screams frustration to the wind,
but no one can hear; she is alone.
So she scourers the beach with salt
filled eyes
And strain with all she has in a direction
not yet tried.
He whispered "don't stop" to her
soggy soul, giving CPR to her hope that
has died.
Hands bleeding and wrinkled clothes
shredded and tattered

All that pales in this moonlight, only
survival matters.
She sees the fin of a shark, thinking he
has a sure meal
Good, I love sushi...come closer and see
your teeth meet an iron will.
Because today, she will not die.
Though she is in a leaky boat tossed
about in this storm
This is not the end of her story; this is not
why she was born.
Every flash of lightning shows her
another picture of the coast
Highlighting the reef and rocks; the
reasons that she can't come to shore.
But He see's something that they can't
show me
He sees that within me...there is more.
More deeds to be performed, more
people to be reached
More testimonies to be told, so she will
make it to that beach.
This is a very dangerous situation
It's as hopeless as a sucker's bet, and she's
much to near to dying
But He reminded her not to forget...to
always...no matter what...keep on trying.

The Significant Dreamer:

The vicissitudes of life
are the mandates
for elevation...

The unspoken proclamations...
Levied on the backbone of promises
Dreams...
Once deferred
'yet I heard
And God confirmed
... you are SIGNFICANT
.... you are THE DREAMER

Remember me
In the midst of
...pit-iful adversity
At that place of levity...
At the point of one's
greatest despair
When you think
... I'm not there
Look up to me
...and see
I will send
Three... Over
Three days

A
...Death
...Burial
...Resurrection
Life thereafter

Yes! SHE matters
... She is SIGNFICANT
... She is THE DREAMER

HER dreams
Cannot
Conflict
Compete
Sleep...
Be diminished
Only finished...
... She is SIGNFICANT
... She is THE DREAMER

New testaments
Described issues
Old testaments
Needed tissue...

While they will
Try to repudiate her
Stand and instead

Divulge the gifts within her
And without
Repentance
Leave her naysayers
... Obstructed
Unblended by justice

Ah...
At last
Silence...
Sssh....
Listen...
For they speak freely
Never needing to
Know me...
Redefined by the
Inner me
Not her enemy
And as God
Reminds thee....
... She is SIGNFICANT
... She is THE DREAMER

Corrected the inner critic
Eliminated the cloud of doubt
Shouted, screamed, stomped it out

Like that broken down train
She thinks she can
She knows she can
She can…. DO…………… ALL………
THINGS……….
For her place isn't with the people
But in the presence of… THE… King Yes!
My Daughter
… She is SIGNFICANT
… She is THE DREAMER

Purposely designed
In His mind's eye

Not for the
… Noble prize
… Purple heart
… Light at the end of the tunnel
…. Commendation
… Sideline conversations

Let it be no surprise
She will bring about
Divine manifestation
Propel the masses
To their ultimate destination

For the...
 Baker prepared it
Cupbearer served it
She dreamt it
He manifested it...

...She is SIGNIFICANT
...She is THE DREAMER

She Speaks

CHAPTER TWO

The Conception of Joseph:

Granddad Carlos's successful days running black market numbers on Jefferson street had finally paid off, equipping him with the financial ability to move the Duson family out of the dilapidated conditions of 31 Welker street, into a bigger home near the west side of city, 920 Lafayette. Grandma Anita, a confessed racist, quickly became known by neighbors and passersby's throughout the neighborhood as the nosy, grumpy old woman who sat in her window day after day spewing racial slurs. She spoke only to black people, verbally degrading them, especially when any white person or person lighter than she, walked by. It wasn't long before she got comfortable in her surroundings, and it was an even shorter period of time, before she'd put away her phony act of kindness, settling back into her old abusive ways.

Although the exact date of my conception is unknown, the beginning of my story starts here. My conception, which is presumed to have taken place sometime in the fall of 1975, was yet another tragic moment in my mother's life. Barely eighteen, the tall, petite, cocoa-skinned girl with long legs, flowing hair, and striking beauty who had previously escaped the confines of 31 Welker and now, 920 Lafayette, was struggling with her internal demons. She had long since succumbed to drugs, fast money, and prostitution at the hands of good ole, Bernard, and her lifestyle began to wreak its effects on her.

While working the streets one night, my mother's pimp, William "Bernard" Griffith, decided that he wanted to have her, but he didn't intend to pay for her services. He raped my mother, igniting flashbacks of my mother's tragic encounter some six years back. My mother wanted to run to someone...anyone, but knowing that she had been gone so long, she was unsure as to just where or who to run to. She was certain that she couldn't return home to my grandmother. In my mother's mind, harboring the trauma stemming from the rape was emotional torture in and of itself. The last thing she needed was Grandma Anita adding even more torture. So even though weeks eventually passed without secure refuge, my mother remained steadfast in her determination not to return to the place she once called home.

About a month after the rape, my mother received what she referred to as, *'the blow'*—she was carrying her rapist's seed. In her eyes, giving birth to the child would be a constant reminder of the violation, abuse, and tragedy—the same curses she had tried to bury and put behind her.

During this time, abortions were available, but they were too expensive and not a common practice in the African-American community. If my mother could have, though, she would have aborted me. My only saving grace was her poverty and her pimp, who refused to pay for what he considered "the cost of doing business".

"You ain't the first trick to get knocked up, and you won't be the last," Bernard said, after she told him about her pregnancy.

"What am I supposed to do?" my mother asked, hoping he'd offer at least some means of assistance.

"Look, like I told you, you ain't the first trick to get knocked up. Do what the other tricks do, have the little bastard, but don't think it'll be calling me daddy or anything like it. Y'all are on your own."

So with limited options, my mother returned to her aunt, Patricia's, apartment. That decision, however, came with a price—having to live with Patricia's unconventional rules. But my mother wasn't putting up a fight, since she needed her rest and was on strict orders from the doctor to take things easy for the next few weeks.

∞ ∞ ∞ ∞

Several weeks later, my Aunt Patricia convinced my mother to attend a Sunday breakfast at their parents' house. Despite the many negative things she was known for, my grandmother was infamous for her buffet-style meals fit to feed an army—grits, eggs, bacon, toast, the works.

They were greeted by the familiar sound of Grandma Anita's voice echoing through the house when they walked in the house.

"Hurry up and get your asses in here now, so you can eat! Yawl got thirty seconds, and if you don't get in here, then your asses are outta luck!"

The sounds and scurries of feet down the stairs followed. Family meals were not that frequent, so the opportunity to join together as a family was rare but seen as an opportunity to bond, in the Duson family way, which meant bland conversation, for the most part, and idle dialogue. But for what it was worth, it seemed to work for the Dusons.

"I saw fish in my dream the other night," my grandmother said, in between chews.

Typically, dreaming of fish, in the black community, is symbolic of someone in the family because pregnant.

Suddenly, the room became stoically quiet, particularly the girls, as their eyes focused in on each other. My mother couldn't keep her secret inside. She saw the silence as an opportune time to make the dreaded announcement.

"I'm pregnant," she blurted out.

"Aww, hell naw, yo ugly ass ain't pregnant!" my grandmother laughed. "Who would want to have a child with you?"

My mother sat in silence as all eyes were glued on her. My grandmother's demeanor changed once reality set in. She glared at my mother, looking as if she wanted start wailing on her at any second.

"Your ass better not bring no damn child up in here! If your ass is grown enough to lie down and make a baby, then you're grown enough to get your ass out there and take care of it on your own. I done raised all the children I'm going to raise. I am not having or raising no more."

My mother's eyes watered. "I was raped, Momma," she embarrassingly confessed. "A man who calls himself 'Bernard' did it."

Quick as a flash, my grandmother reached over and smacked my mother in the head so hard that my mother fell back in her chair. "Shut your god***n mouth!" she hissed. "I don't ever want to hear that shit again! If you wasn't out there hoeing around, you wouldn't be in this god***n situation!"

Grabbing a hold to the chair legs, my mother mustered the strength to lift herself off the floor. She stood up, gained her balance, and ran out of the dining room. Grandma Anita followed right behind her while an eerie silence fell over the dining room table again. Not knowing what else to do, everyone at the table continued to eat their food, being forced to listen to my mother's wails and screams as my grandmother beat, stomped, cursed, and kicked her around upstairs.

"I'll beat that baby outta you!"

"Mama, please!" my mother begged, trying to get my grandmother to stop.

"Get yo ass out, and don't ever come back!"

So my mother left 920 Lafayette that day disheveled and confused. Somehow, the only thing intact was her pregnancy; her self-esteem had hit its lowest level in all of her years and her faith in God and everyone else had seemingly disappeared into oblivion. It was then that my mother made up in her mind that she would persevere, nonetheless, using this devastating experience as a catalyst for a lifestyle change.

With the aid of welfare, Medicaid, and food stamps, my mother was able to get up on her feet, so to speak. Unfortunately, however, she wasn't receiving enough money to take care of herself, at least not at the rate she was used to. In her pregnant state, she reverted back to the streets, and good ole Bernard, despite his earlier rejection, was there with open arms and a whole new bag of tricks. It wasn't long before my mother found herself once again 'employed' in the streets.

Christmas rolled around that year, and my mother who didn't act like a woman with child, would find herself all alone. She literally lived in the streets, bouncing back and forth between associates—johns who pretended to care—in exchange for free sex, as well as men she slept with for money and heroin, the drug of choice for many prostitutes.

Shockingly, she managed to get through the following spring without incident and slowly tried to pull herself together as the time was growing closer for her to give birth. With the money she received from welfare as well as her other resources, she had surprisingly saved up enough money to move into a rundown apartment on the west side of the city. She turned to her father for extra help. He took some of the money that he hustled from the street numbers and assisted her with some of the more basic necessities like bedroom furniture, baby clothes, a crib, a television, and a couch. He begged her not to tell her mother that he had helped her out, because he knew that if Grandma Anita found out, she would have thrown him out as well.

"Now, you can't tell your mother I'm helping you. It'll wreak havoc in the house, and both of our heads will be on her chopping block," he cautioned.

Granddad Carlos merely wanted to somehow keep the peace, although he was conflicted by his allegiance to Grandma Anita as the man of the house and his duty to help his daughter and unborn grandchild.

∞ ∞ ∞ ∞

On June 1, 1976, my mother arose in the middle of the night, saturated in a pool of clear fluid. Assuming she hadn't lost control of her bladder, she dialed 911 and was transported to Millard Fillmore Hospital.

Finally, at 11:41 pm, after some fourteen plus hours of intensive labor, and despite her neglect of prenatal care, my mother pushed out a 6 pound, 9 ounce, and 17-inch long baby girl—me. After the doctor had suctioned out her lungs, the wail of a survivor was heard—mine—whose life would begin in tragedy. I was a frail, yet healthy baby with all ten fingers and toes and had a head that was slightly big, yet full of jet black, silky hair. I was described as a baby who, like most, slept all the time and stayed relatively quiet. Granddad Carlos stopped by as often as possible during the first week after I was born. My aunties sent gifts through him because they were afraid of what Grandma Anita would say or do if she got wind of their visits. She put the fear of God in my aunts and uncles, causing them to keep their distance from both my mother and me. Although everyone was curious to see me, they diverted their attention instead to my cousin, Garry, Aunt Denise's only child, who had been born seven months earlier on Halloween. Like before, Grandma Anita selected the male, Garry, to be the person she would show favor upon, and me, to be the recipient of her anger.

Granddad Carlos chalked it up to Grandma Anita being stubborn.

"She'll come around," Granddad Carlos assured my mother.

From the very beginning, Granddad Carlos was my savior. He gave me the nickname "Tiffer" to distinguish between me and three other Tiffanys that lived in the neighborhood, making the claim that I would be his angel forever. However, after I was only one week old, Granddad Carlos told my mother that he would not be able to come around for a while because Grandma Anita was on his case about his whereabouts. He had run out of lies, and, although my mother was his flesh and blood, he had to be the peacekeeper, making sure the ice queen stayed happy.

With that news and the mounting responsibilities of being a single mom, week two of my life proved extremely emotional for my mother. She was experiencing the "baby blues" in a bad way. Feelings of destitution set in, and, with no visitors to check in on her or distract her; her drug usage increased and she fell into a deep depression. She reconnected with ole Bernard, who this time, pulled yet some even newer tricks from his bag, causing my mother to resort to an increased use of heroin and marijuana in exchange for personally servicing him. Needless to say, things spiraled out of control in her world. Just looking at me constantly reminded her of the brutal attack that August night. She was broke, had no food, and could no longer afford to take care of me, financially, much less provide any means of emotional support. To add to her despair, her family had turned its collective back on her, and Granddad Carlos, although he loved us both, had been forced to step out of the picture.

All lifelines were depleted and life seemed hopeless for my mother. It was these elements combined that caused her to abandon me. She packed a bag with everything she could grab and headed for the nearest Greyhound bus station. With less than one hundred dollars in her pocket, she hopped aboard the first bus she could get on. Three days later, she would turn up in Seattle, Washington—alone, leaving me three thousand miles behind, locked in the bedroom of a hot apartment.

Ms. Moore, an elderly, widowed woman known for her no-nonsense kind of demeanor, had become good friends with Granddad Carlos, lived adjacent to us. Unbeknown to my mother, Granddad Carlos had secretly asked Ms. Moore to keep an eye on us. They would often stand on the sidewalk and chit chat during Granddad Carlos visits.

"Watch my gal," he would always say to Ms. Moore before he left my mother's apartment.

"You betcha," she always assured.

So in keeping up with her promise, she'd often come by and check in on my mother. Knowing my mother's personality, I'm sure she deemed Ms. Moore as a nosy old lady, but Ms. Moore was merely adhering to Granddad Carlos's request.

Needless to say, Ms. Moore had become worried after nearly five days had passed and she realized that she had not seen my mother or even heard any normal sounds of life coming from our apartment—no sounds coming from the television, no sounds coming from the squeaky water pipe when the toilet flushed, no arguments between my mother and Bernard, no sounds of a crying baby, no strange bursts of laughter followed by eerie sounds of silence coming from my mother when she was on her drug binges, nothing. So she decided to check in on us. She knocked on the door and rang the doorbell repeatedly but got no response. The complete silence—no background chatter, no noise from the television, running water, or voice of a crying newborn—worried her. She found a rock lying on the side of our cracked concrete that led to our apartment and threw it through the front door window. She reached her hand in and unlocked the door from the inside. She turned the knob and pushed the door open. A gush of heat and the scent of urine and fecal matter seemed strong enough to singe the hair in her nostrils.

Ms. Moore canvassed the apartment like a detective, noticing used syringes on the on the coffee table, molded food on the counter, dirty towels thrown about in the bathroom, and swarming flies coming from the back of the apartment.

"Conitra," she called out to my mother. In all honesty, she probably wasn't expecting for my mother to respond. She was basically operating on auto-pilot. In her gut, she knew my mother was long gone. She stood still for a moment, thinking about how she would deliver the news to Granddad Carlos. It was in that moment that she heard faint wailing sounds coming from the back of the apartment. She followed the sounds until it led her to the back bedroom. She slowly turned the doorknob, pushed the bedroom door open and found me lying nearly unconscious on the bed in my own vomit, urine, and feces. Frantically, she rushed over to the bed, scooped me up, and ran next door to her own apartment. She immediately phoned Granddad Carlos and broke the news to him.

"What do you want me to do with her? I mean, she looks like she's in bad condition. Even her breath sounds seem weak," Ms. Moore said, inspecting me from head to toe.

"Drop her off at my house," Granddad Carlos instructed.

Although somewhat perplexed by Granddad Carlos's request and his overall reaction, she did as he instructed and placed me in a basket and dropped me at 920 Lafayette. She left me in the hallway in front of the door, rang the doorbell, and left, without waiting for anyone answer. Cousin Antoine opened the door and discovered me in the basket in the hallway, now unconscious.

With the luxury of being able to attend to me because Grandma Anita was not home, he sent Antoine to the restroom to get a warm towel and washed my face, trying to at least tone down the smell of vomit and feces on me. Afterward, he and Antoine rushed me to Millard Fillmore Hospital at Gates Circle. The ER doctors attempted to revive me. I gained consciousness at some point, but the medical staff did convey to my granddad that my odds weren't looking too good. With knowledge of my abandonment, the authorities were then notified, and within a matter of hours, warrants for my mother's arrest were issued. She was officially being charged with reckless endangerment, child abandonment, neglect, and abuse. But my mother was long gone, and no one even knew here to look for her.

Granddad Carlos remained at my bedside, praying for God to spare my life. At some point, Child Protective Services came onto the scene. They wanted to take custody of me. They gave my granddad an ultimatum—either a member of the family would have to take custody of me within ten days, or I would become a ward of the State and be placed up for adoption.

For many years, I wished that Granddad Carlos would have allowed the State to take custody. Perhaps my life would have been very different, for the better. But since we were in the same hospital where my mother had given birth to me, her next of kin was on record. Child Protective Services contacted my Grandma Anita.

They gave her the same ultimatum that they had given Granddad Carlos. Even though she had no true intentions in doing so, Grandma Anita told the social worker that she would have to confer with her husband and get back to them. Reality was that there was no way she was going to take me in nor allow my Granddad Carlos to do so.

But this time, unlike many times before, Granddad Carlos stood up to Grandma Anita.

"If she goes, I'm going, too," he said.

Taken aback my Granddad Carlos's stance, Grandma Anita did what she hadn't done in the past—she conceded and allowed Granddad Carlos to take full custody of me.

I remained in the hospital for another three weeks, gained back all the weight I had lost, and, aside from the minor scars, everything about me was pretty normal. I was released from the hospital in mid-September, and, even though my grandmother had agreed to be my guardian, she was not the one that showed up to the hospital on my day of discharge. Granddad Carlos arrived at my bedside with bells and whistles in tote to carry me home—the same place that had represented a palace of misery for my mother.

When we arrived at 920 Lafayette, granddad had a surprise waiting for me—a three-pound German Shepherd puppy named Sonny. Sonny and I were the newest arrivals to the household and we soon became inseparable. The family pet was now my best friend. Like a budding relationship, in the beginning all seemed well. It appeared that maybe, just maybe, I'd be welcomed into the home. The house was huge, and a bunch of us lived there—my cousins, Antoine, Marie, and Garry, and my Aunts Theresa and Denise.

Garry and Marie were Grandma Anita's favorites, and she made no bones admitting it or displaying more affection to them than she did to me. Even still, my life at the time was as ordinary as any newborn baby's; however, my peaceful "goo-goo-gaga" moments would be the only peaceful childhood memories I'd ever have. As I got older, things changed, for the worse, unfortunately.

The 1976 holiday season was upon us. Thanksgiving came, and, as always, Grandma Anita prepared a huge feast. She managed to put my mother's absence out of her mind, resigning herself to the fact that for the time being she was stuck with me. Most of the family was there, and it was an exciting time. For a snapshot moment in time, we were a picture- perfect family. Marie and Antoine were transitioning from elementary to middle school, and then, from middle school to junior high. Antoine, though, was still being abused by Anita physically and emotionally and simultaneously, being molested by a male friend of the family who was associated with Uncle Dennis. Aware of the molestation, Anita chose not to address it. So Antoine remained silent, living a torturous life like my mother did in so many ways.

At Thanksgiving there was so much food. Grandma Anita was a gourmet pastry chef, and her southern roots enabled her to throw together a meal in her kitchen better than that in the movie "Soul Food." At Thanksgiving, everything was prepared from scratch. She'd toast up loaves of Wonder Bread, make cornbread from scratch for her infamous stuffing, wash collard greens and season them to perfection, prepare macaroni and cheese with at least four different kinds of cheese, boil and whip mashed potatoes by hand with gravy made of flour, water, and her secret spices, and, of course, her infamous turkey was quite juicy and tender. This celebration came with great anticipation, because the food and fun wouldn't last afterward.

After the big feast, Grandma Anita pulled out her white Christmas tree, in commemoration for what would be the first Christmas at 920 Lafayette. Granddad Carlos decorated both the inside and outside of the house with lights, and the older children were assigned the tasks of decorating the tree and cleaning up afterward.

For some unknown reason, the weather patterns began to change in December of that year. Lake Erie had frozen over, an early record that year. The freezing of the lake had normally put an end to the lake effect snowstorms created by winds picking up moisture from the lake surface, converting it to snow, and dumping it when those winds reached shore. This winter, though, was different. Oddly enough, we appeared functional. Christmas came, and all the kids were delightfully surprised. Granddad Carlos's hustle afforded him to splurge, sparing no expense on his family that year. The Duson's were always known for having money, so we typically enjoyed the holidays.

A compulsive neat freak, Grandma Anita would rise before all of us at 5:00 am and clean the house spotless. Our house had the reputation as being the cleanest and best-decorated house on the block. Coupled with the white winters Buffalo was associated with, from outside it was a picture perfect home for a postcard; but the inside held dark secrets. On Christmas Eve, we would be put to bed shortly after nine, and then the adults would bring the gifts out of hiding. The children had no qualms about waking up at six o'clock in the morning. There was sheer excitement for the children, but a growing disappointment for me, as I would soon discover the difference in the distribution of gift.

When it came to actual celebration time, which were usually centered around meals, the children were given baked cookies, hard cider, tons of candy, and orange foam peanuts, while the adults would drink hard cider, spiked with their cognac of choice, and indulge in their grownup conversations.

For me, these were the only times of year that bore any hint of normalcy, or at least gave the appearance thereof. Our family came from all over to celebrate Christmas, both blood and extended, and yet two people,

in my mind's eye, were missing, and no one ever openly reminisced or spoke of them. Although I was young,
I must have, at some point, wondered, *Where were my
mom and dad, and why was I there without them?* Those
questions were never answered.

By late January, with the holidays now behind us,
the snow depth in Buffalo grew from thirty to thirty-five
inches, and street plowing was already falling behind—
thirty-three of the city's seventy-nine plows were in for
repairs. More ominously, snow depth on the ten thousand square miles of Lake Erie's surface was almost at
three feet. Although the National Weather Service had
posted blizzard warnings, that fateful Friday, January
28, 1977, started out quite pleasant. There was little
wind, and it wasn't too cold for late January. Suddenly,
though, just before noon the infamous Blizzard of '77 hit.

The temperature quickly plummeted to near zero,
and the winds arrived with gusts peaking at more than
seventy miles per hour. This produced a wind chill that
nearly dropped off the chart, to almost sixty degrees
below zero. Only about fifteen feet of new snow fell
over the next several days, but western New York and
nearby Canada were also inundated with tons of
snow blown in off Lake Erie. As a consequence, vis-
ibility remained at zero for the first twenty-five hours
of the storm. Drivers found themselves being buried,
and many, surrounded by the whiteout, were forced
to stay in their cars. Some of these persons contribut-

ed to the death toll of twenty-nine, having died of dying of carbon monoxide poisoning or exposure. Hearing of people marooned in their cars, police struggled over drifts to bang on car roofs. They were relieved if no one answered because they had no way of digging them out.

Although there was some looting and theft during the storm, it was mostly an episode that brought the community together. Stores, restaurants, and hotels provided food and places to stay, often free. Agencies such as the Salvation Army and the Red Cross as well as city

and county departments, worked continuously throughout the emergency to provide services and temporary
refuge. Individuals not only helped neighbors but strangers as well.

The blizzard extended to February 1, 1977. Granddad Carlos would brave daily wind gusts that ranged
from forty-six to sixty-nine mph in order to get his
hustle on. But we survived the Blizzard of 77, and everything would appear somewhat normal for the next three
and a half years.

Sometime during my fourth year of life, the neglect
and abuse began. It started off subtle; nonetheless, by
the time I was five years old, the brash of beatings would
intensify, causing my vivid memories to become not so
pleasant. The only safe times were during the holidays
and family gatherings, particularly Thanksgiving and
Christmas. They were the only times during the year
that I felt like I belonged. All other times, I was mistreat-
ed and abused. I longed for the day when love would tuck
me in the bed at night, wake me up in the morning, and
stay with me throughout the day; a day when my mother
would return and take me into arms and tell me it would
be all right. She didn't have to apologize; I would have
settled for her presence along. But none of these things
happened, at least not for a very long time, leaving me to
wonder for many years, *Why me?*

I miss her...

She who was my what, where and when
She who was fresh as the newly tilled
ground...before the seeds of sin
And find myself searching the eyes of
other lost souls...who wander lost streets
And I cry out daily for an answer...but no
answer greets
So I just miss...having the option...
to deliver my first kiss
Having a mind that does not doubt why
I am born into this
Of lovely days of courting a boy that
surprises me with his charm
Of just one doctor in the family...that
believed in "do no harm"

Like a vessel I am always full...and trying
not to tip too far left or right
I just want to have stability
I want a place that I can be safe
I want the memories that you have
And to burn the ones that I carry
For those are too real for most to be able
to handle
Just give me a match...cuz I long ago lost
my candle

And my picture on the milk carton, just
got thrown away
I now envy, whatever your first thought
was...when u awoke today
Want me to tell what my mind
downloaded this am?
The shame of the prostitute, without the
obligation to pay 'em
Just slay her womanhood...and kill all
that she held dear
Grind down her options...while releasing
all her fears
And watch what she becomes...her
disfigured and stunted growth
No foundation to anything good...spilled
blood, her only kept oath
Words cannot describe the depth of
longing...to one day be history free
I guess what I'm trying to say is that
I miss the "Her". That still resides in me

CHAPTER THREE

Innocence Lost:

Naked came I out of my mother's womb, and naked shall I return thither: the LORD gave, and the LORD hath taken away; blessed be the name of the Lord. ~Job 1:21

Job is my favorite Old Testament book. It is most interpretive in addressing the perplexing questions that might be raised while reading this next chapter, particular the question as to why the righteous suffer. How ironic that the adversities of Job actually seem to be a part of the human dilemma today. However, man has the treasure of life (incorruptible, immortal, glorious, and powerful) in an earthen vessel (corruptible, mortal, infamy, and weak). What happens when man violates this innocence? Do you give up and die? No, as Job did, you simply persevere.

∞ ∞ ∞ ∞

On a cool, crisp September morning in 1981, I was preparing to enter kindergarten. I remember looking down at my new shoes, doing the Cinderella step, curious and excited at the same time. Granddad Carlos had found the best school money could buy. He paid for both me and Garry to attend the Diocesan Education Center (D.E.C.), a Catholic School on Buffalo's east side, which is where the children of Buffalo's middle and upper classes were schooled. The brick edifice had four floors, including a basement, and was adorned with arch-styled windows from the front to the back. In its day, it was an educational force to be reckoned with.

We weren't rich, but Granddad Carlos spared no expense when it came to our education. It's ironic when I think about it today because on one hand, I was given some of the best things. In this case, a quality education. On the other hand, I was given some of the worst things—mistreatment, beatings, and excessive punishments. Nevertheless, on my first day of school, Grandma Anita escorted me. I vividly remember walking across a marred concrete parking lot down a set of stairs. At the bottom of the stairs to my left was a dimly lit tunnel, which was a passageway to the cafeteria, the annexed junior high school, and the upper classrooms. The passageway also served as a recess area where the kids would hang out between classes to chit-chat or show off their latest breakdancing moves. To the right of the stairs was a section of kindergarten classes, including mine.

Grandma Anita had coached me on everything I was supposed to say and do on this very important day. Before she opened the door to my classroom, she tested my remembrance.

"What's your name?" Grandma asked, with her right hand on the doorknob.

"Tiffany Marie Duson," I said with confidence. I had practiced saying my name for the past week so I wouldn't fail the task. I was certain that there'd be consequences if I did.

She looked me over with her wide eyes, as she'd always do when she was looking to find fault. Not fully pleased with my appearance, she wet her fingers with her saliva and wiped the corners of my mouth, a behavior I always found squeamishly repulsive. She crouched down until she was eyelevel with me. "You get in there and do what your teachers tell you to do! Keep your mouth shut about things that ain't that "white-man's" business, and don't let none of them children get to playing in your hair. You hear me, little gal?"

"Yes...yes ma'am," I replied.

She turned the doorknob and opened the door. I walked into class with those instructions and quietly took my seat. Grandma Anita waved goodbye to me from the door. I read her lips, "Have great day." My eyes followed Grandma Anita as she turned and walked away until I could no longer see the image of the flowery-patterned dress sashaying down the hallway.

Kindergarten proved to be uneventful. I passed with flying colors and rave reviews, collecting gold stars and A's across the board. I was flooded with compliments from my teacher and administration about how bright I was, although I didn't quite understand the term "bright". I was under the impression that it meant I was sort of special. I did understand one thing, though— I was smart, and, combined with being special, I figured it must have really counted for something because everyone outside of 920 Lafayette was talking about me.

Meanwhile, those inside 920 Lafayette made it a ritual to talk about how much of a disgrace I was, or how I was the bastard child to my mother.

"She's gon' be just like Conitra, you watch and see," I heard Grandma Anita say to Aunt Denise one day while Aunt Denise was styling Grandma Anita's hair for some party she and Granddad Carlos were attending.

"And that no good daddy of hers, too...whoever he is," Aunt Denise added, after which, the two of them shared hilarious laughter.

I heard comments like these often. But even at that young age, I was considered to be resilient. I was determined to move beyond my circumstances and become someone great, proving Grandma Anita and the others wrong.

Time flew by rapidly, and before I knew it, I was graduating and preparing to advance to First Grade. For graduation, I got the works—new dress, new shoes, and a new hairstyle. Cousin Marie braided my hair in box braids and decorated the ends with blue and white beads to match my cap and gown. I'd shake my hair profusely just to hear the sounds the beads made. My class rehearsed Whitney Houston's song, "The Greatest Love of All", over and over again until we perfected it. On the big day, the entire family was present— Grandma Anita, my aunts, and my many cousins. We appeared to be a normal, healthy family by pulling off the façade of unity, with incessant clapping and cheering. Even as a six-year old, I was very aware that we were living a lie before our neighbors and friends. At the same time, I knew that our secret was meant to be kept.

That summer, was a precedent of what my following summers would be like. Instead of having a carefree summer, I was made to sit at the dining room table to practice my penmanship and read books selected by Grandma Anita, in preparation to enter my second year at D.E.C. Many days, I would find myself in a daze, starring out of the dirty dining room front window, watching Garry run up and down Lafayette Street playing with his friends. Although I viewed him as a hellion, a true instigator, I longed to trade places with him many of those summer days just to enjoy being a kid. Outside of these specific incidences, I wouldn't want to trade places with Garry. He was brat and was responsible for many of my punishment and beatings, including having been dragged across the living room floor by Grandma Anita.

Sundays were not the typical "go-to-church" day in the Duson home. They were much like all the other days, at least for me. Grandma Anita would make me lie still in the bed for hours and practice my handwriting skills over and over, after which, I had to clean the house, do laundry, help cook, and then, clean some more. On the rare occasion that I was able to steal some "me" time, I wrote in a journal and read books. By the time I was seven, I was reading books like *To Kill a Mocking-*

bird and other titles that were categorized as teenage and adult material.

While we didn't go to church on Sundays, the house was lively at an early hour. Being a very early bird, I used to wake up and sneak a quarter of the way downstairs. I could always hear Grandma Anita the kitchen talking to herself, crying and laughing, too, but all the while asking God, "When ya gonna bring ya chile on home?" She'd continue to talk to herself and God for a while and even answer herself, which I found strange but amusing, nonetheless. I'd sit on the stairs, peering through the railings, watching and listening to her ramblings, which included a prayer for all her children and grandchildren. Once she finished, that was my cue. She would yell upstairs for me. Naturally, I'd wait a few moments, pretending to be just getting up, before coming down to answer her call. "Go on and turn the radio on," she'd say. "Find my gospel show."

Although I found much of what Grandma Anita did to be what the grown-ups back then referred to as "the devil's work," she did show, albeit it was very miniscule in nature, she had some form of a God conscious. But I would do what I was told and find the radio station, often just in time for us to hear Shirley Caesar singing "No Charge," Grandma Anita's favorite song.

"We are good Catholic Christians," she'd say. "Jesus is everywhere, baby gal, and we ain't about to go to nobody's church to find 'em."

Then she'd start singing so loud that Aunt Denise would wake up and stomp on the floor above our head, signaling for Grandma Anita to shut up.

"Aww go da hell! Stop dat shit! Yo ass needs some prayers," she'd holler in retaliation. "Get yo lazy ass outta dat bed. If ya don't like it, then yo ass can find the door. Grown ass woman still in her momma's house. No charge, godda***t!" Grandma Anita would charge. She definitely had a comeback the majority of the time. Strangely enough, that was probably the one thing that I secretly admired about her.

After she finished ranting, Grandma Anita would continue singing as if nothing had transpired moments before. She'd begin preparing breakfast, with me passing the eggs and retrieving the milk and cooking utensils in an effort to make myself helpful. I would watch her every move to learn how I could later emulate her soulful cooking. Once everything was ready, I would run upstairs and wake everyone else for breakfast.

Granddad Carlos was always the first one down. He'd immediately go out the door to grab the paper and head to the backyard to feed my dog. I'd get the coupons section from him so he could clip them for Grandma Anita after he perused through his two favorite sections—the lotto numbers and sports. When everyone finally made it downstairs, we'd all gather around the table. Grandma Anita would say a short prayer, and, on cue, plates would pass. This was also the opportune time for Grandma Anita to perform another one of her customary rituals—bashing the family. She'd start in on Aunt Denise, usually still drunk from the previous night. It would usually go something like this.

"I'm tired of you bringing yo drunk ass up in here. Grown ass people need their own place! God bless the chile that got her own," she continued, slightly misquoting the infamous song sang by Billie Holiday.

"And God said let thee be skinny," Aunt Denise retaliated. Aunt Denise's only mode of attack on Grandma Anita was to talk about her weight. Sure she was a bit thick, but she wore it pretty well.

"Well, your white pimp like it," Grandma Anita said, with a slight grin on her face. She knew it would really get Aunt Denise in a tizzy.

One particular Sunday, Granddad Carlos had finally had enough of their back and forth. "Shut the hell up," he demanded, looking at both Grandma Anita and Aunt Denise. This was a first for him. But almost instantly, there was silence. Granddad had boldly taken charge by wielding his influence over Grandma Anita. It was an odd moment, since he had rarely taken the onus to check Grandma Anita's authority before.

She glared at him. "Who the hell are you talking to?"

"You, dammit!" Granddad Carlos answered.

Granddad Carlos's boldness excited me. Finally someone had stood up to Grandma Anita. I knew he was not just my ally, but more like my savior. I could really trust Granddad Carlos. If Grandma Anita got on me while he was home, he would be there to save me from her brutal whooping. So as I lay in the bed that night, the recurring questions that I've always wanted to know the answers to but was too scared to ask, consumed my mind once again. Where was my mommy? Who's my daddy? Why did she leave me?

The next morning, I rose with some of those very questions on my mind. While I was practicing my penmanship, curiosity got the best of me. When Grandma Anita came in the room to check my work, I just went for it.

"Where's my mommy?"

"Who?" Grandma Anita asked, not sure she had heard me correctly.

"My mommy? And who's my daddy?"

Grandma Anita put my paper down. She appeared to think for a minute before answering me. "I don't know where your mammy is. She ran off a long time ago. I believe she's somewhere out west." She stopped for a moment, as if she was reliving the incident. "But she don't have the decency to call or send you a card, which means she don't give a damn. So do me a favor and don't ever ask about her ass again!" she continued, with her voice and disposition seemingly gaining increasing volume and venom.

What had started out as a gentle explanation suddenly changed. I sat still, scared to move or ask another question. Not only was I scared, I was more puzzled than anything.

"Oh, and yo daddy was a bad man. He did some horrible things to your mammy. But if ya ask me, she got what she deserved. First, she f**ked around and got her throat slit from left to right, then got left for dead. Second, she shouldn't have been in those streets, sellin' her ass," Grandma Anita continued, acting as though the punishment fit the crime.

She grew quiet once again. Then, she turned back to me and slapped me upside my head. "Finish your damn writing and stop asking so many godda*n questions!"

Distraught and hurt all at the same time, I didn't utter another word. I was glad that she ended the story as abruptly as she did. As a matter fact, I didn't want to hear another word.

On top of how she had originally felt about me and my mother, my having the audacity to ask legitimate questions about my parents, Grandma Anita had it in for me like never before. When I came in from outside this particular afternoon, Grandma Anita was sitting in her raggedy green recliner behind the front door. She beckoned for me to come.

"Come here," she said in that stern voice I knew signaled trouble. "Let me look you over."

Thinking nothing of it, I rushed over to her and stood erect in front of her, with my chest stuck out proudly for a quick look over.

Without saying a word, she balled her fingers into a tight fist and swung at me with all her might. Her fist landed square in my chest. I fell to the floor, banging my shoulder on the cocktail table on the way down. Now, that's what I called knocking the life out of someone.

"W-w-what did I do?" I managed to utter, in a low whisper. I had no idea where the increased rage had come from. I usually saw the whooping coming, but this one took me completely by surprise.

"Shut the hell up before I give you something else to cry about!" she yelled.

I wanted to comply, but I couldn't control my tears, and I couldn't breathe. As best as I knew, I hadn't done anything I shouldn't have. But I couldn't help but wonder, *Why else would she slap me?*

Grandma Anita she stood up.

"Bring yo ass here," she growled.

I hesitated. Nothing in her voice sounded good, and I certainly didn't want to get hit again. My hesitation proved to be a bad decision. Anita bent down, grabbed my legs, and dragged me across the carpet, ripping my tights and irritating old rug burns from previous episodes of being dragged across the floor.

"Get up," she said, continuing to punch, slap, and kick me.

I tried to get up, but her licks were coming at me so fast, I couldn't see straight. I certainly didn't have the strength to withstand her punches in my face, back, chest, and abdomen. I was no match for her, physically.

Suddenly, she stopped. Just like that. Granddad Carlos had not come to save me. In fact, he wasn't home. Had he been, this wouldn't have happened.

Just like that, she appeared to be done—at least that's what I thought.

"Get yo ass up dem stairs and wait. I'll be right there," she said, storming out of the front room. This usually meant she was looking for some props—a broom, a frying pan, a skillet, a pair of shoes, an extension cord—anything she could get her hands on.

Her words went through me like an electric shock. My feet barely touched the stairs as I flew up them and headed straight for my room. I knew the routine—strip down to my underwear and wait. There was no one in the house but me and Grandma Anita. I waited for what seemed like hours before Grandma Anita finally came upstairs.

"What did I tell you about playing in your hair?" she said walking close to me, in slow motion, it seemed.

"We were playing. I didn't—" Those were the only words I could get out of my mouth before Grandma Anita's backhand came crashing against the side of my face. My head went backwards, hitting the headboard. I crouched into fetal position, trying to protect my face from yet another blow.

"Oh, you think you slick," Grandma Anita said, realizing that she had no open space to knock the daylights out of me once again. She hit me again anyway, and again, and again.

This was the very first time I thought about running to get away from Grandma Anita. *What did I have to lose?* I jumped off the bed and made a go for it. But I got as far as the hallway before she grabbed me by my underwear and dragged me into her bedroom, almost ripping my underwear off in the process.

"Grandma, I didn't do anything. I messed up my own hair playing. I didn't let anybody play in my hair," I pleaded, hoping she'd believe me.

My declarations meant nothing. Grandma Anita was intent on punishing me. She reached into her drawer and pulled out two pairs of pantyhose.

"Sit right here," she demanded, pointing to a spot that was parallel with the footboard of her bed. "Now gimme your feet," she continued, kneeling down on the floor next to me.

I moved my feet, and she pressed them side-by-side, tied them together, and then tied them to the bedpost.

"Now, gimme your hands," she said with not an ounce of trepidation in her voice. She put my hands on top of one another and tied them together. Then, she tied them to the bedpost. She stood up as if to examine her handiwork, pulling on the pantyhose to see if they were tight enough. That is, so I wouldn't be able to escape. "I'll be right back," she said, turning to walk out of her room.

With what seemed like only a few seconds, she returned to the room. This time, she had an extension cord in her hand. She gave no speech. She raised her left hand and went to lashing. My body flinched with each last. At some point in the beating, my flesh began to sting. I couldn't hold the screams back any longer. My wails were incessant—I was crying out for mercy and crying out for death at the same time. In this instant, I just wanted to die. In my fragile mind, life was just too hard and unfair.

The beating itself wasn't the worst part of the ordeal. Grandma Anita didn't untie me right away. Instead, she left me tied to the bed and allowed me to cry myself to sleep. But it must have been the cold draft that woke me sometime in the middle of the night. I was no longer tied the bedpost but lying in fetal position next to it.

I had to virtually peel my underwear off my body. But in effort to hide the brutal beating, especially from Granddad Carlos, Grandma Anita ordered me to take a bath. I gritted my teeth as I lifted my shirt up.

"You better hurry yo ass on up," Grandma Anita yelled from on the other side of the bathroom door.

I took her comment as a threat because at the end of the day, that's essentially what it was. Interpreted, it meant that part three would follow if I didn't hurry it up. So I pressed through the pain and took my underwear off. With a half-bloodied body full of welts and bruises, I stepped into the bath water, my right foot first. It stung at first. Grandma Anita would always prepare my bathwater. She'd fill it with ninety-seven percent hot water and three percent cold water. Then she'd add Epson salt and turpentine. The smell would make my stomach churn.

"You ain't in that tub all the way, little girlie," she added from the other side of the door, waiting to hear the splashing sound of my rear end submerge in the shallow bathwater.

So I counted to ten and then put my left foot in. I slowly crouched down and lowered my bottom into the water, incrementally.

Although I knew Grandma Anita was keeping time, I purposefully allowed myself the space to reflect. I knew that the beating had nothing to do with me having messed up hair. Instead, I knew it was something else deeper, probably something that had to do with my mother. I would never get an honest answer from Grandma Anita, not then and not never.

For the next two years, I was subject to these kinds of horrific beatings. They were instantaneous, and I never really knew when they were coming. Something as simple as not spelling a word right or not finishing all the food on my plate would cause Grandma Anita to "go in" on me. On the rare occasions that Grandma Anita didn't have enough energy to beat me, she punished me by restricting meals and locking me in the basement. Whether I was beaten severely or starved near to death, Grandma Anita put the fear in me to never say a word to anyone about it. And no matter the season, she would force me to wear long sleeves and long pants to ensure that no one saw my bruises, with the exception of very few times when she hit me in the face and left visible evidence.

Once she heard the splash, she would open the bathroom door and enter. Then she would open the linen closet, which was in the bathroom itself, and reach for a bar of Ivory soap. To this very day, the smell of Ivory soap is a staunch reminder of the abuse I suffered at Grandma Anita's hands. Speaking of her hands, with the very hands that beat me only moments earlier, she used to give me an intimate bath. As if nothing had ever happened, she would give me that woman talk.

"See, a woman gotta keep her body clean. She gotta be clean and pure," she would say as she scrubbed my body with the same scrub brush that had been used to clean the house.

When I would get out of the tub, she'd rub my body down with Vaseline and put powder with cornstarch in all my nooks and crannies. Thinking she had hid her crime well, she'd then send me off to bed burning and tingling with bloodshot eyes and raw skin. My only solace was to lie in bed and wait for the comfort that came from hearing the sound of Granddad Carlos's voice when he returned home from running numbers. But the solace was always short lived because Grandma Anita would start right in on him, demanding money and arguing with him over baseless matters. She was one unhappy woman, and everybody in her life were, at some point or another, recipients of her wrath.

∞ ∞ ∞ ∞

There were some moments when Grandma Anita didn't have it in for me. She would allow me to enjoy momentary pleasures.

In June of 1983, a few days after my seventh birthday, Grandma Anita, Aunt Denise, and some other family members and friends were hanging out on the porch doing the usual smoking, drinking, cursing one another out, and gossiping about the neighbors who were not present. I had been allowed outside of the house, and I was elated. Granddad Carlos had purchased a pair of white skates with red stoppers for me, and Cousin Garry had been tasked with teaching me how to skate. The pursuit didn't come without its own challenges, however. We practiced for days until I finally gained enough confidence to steady myself without him. I was extremely happy that I had conquered this new-found skill, and with that level of enthusiasm, I asked Grandma Anita for permission to skate around the block a few times.

"Yes, but check in every few minutes," she said.

Although it was definitely a shock that she was finally granting me some freedom, I didn't wait await around for her to change her mind. I dashed off and skated around the block a couple times, celebrating me independence. I stopped by to see the two other girls named Tiffany who lived on my block. I had to show off my new skills. We chatted for a few minutes before I told them that I had to head back home.

On my third go-around, a stranger approached me. I had never laid eyes on him in our neighborhood before. Since going out was a sheer luxury and privilege to me, excitement was high and my radar was low. I wasn't skeptical of strangers; I was skeptical of relatives. So naïve and totally oblivious to my surroundings, I continued to skate freely, even daring myself to close my eyes. In my mind, this new world, even if it were to be short lived, reflected my imaginations of what it meant to be a kid—carefree, innocent, and loved.

Before I could wander off into La-La Land, I was interrupted by the sound of a man's voice.

"Excuse me, darling—."

I jumped and almost lost my balance. I turned around, slowly, trying to carefully balance myself in the skates. Squinting, I took a quick glance. I didn't know this man. In fact, I had never seen him in our neighborhood before. But there he was, standing there with a pair of faded grey overalls on, a garment of clothing Granddad Carlos wore sometimes. His shoes were a little run down, scuffed badly in the front and a little on the sides. My eyes followed his voice, eventually allowing me to focus in on his face. His dark-skinned face was covered with lots of small holes, craters, we called them, especially his cheeks. He sort of resembled Mr. Charlie, the neighborhood alcoholic. His big, round eyes stared directly into mine. I couldn't help but focus on his bushy eyebrows. I had never quite seen them that thick.

"I...I didn't mean to scare you, but I'm trying to find a store called Bell's. Are you familiar with the area?

Hesitantly, I replied. "I live around the corner," I said, pointing in the direction of my house.

Bell's was our local supermarket, and was not hard to find. But in my naivety, I proceeded to give him directions.

"So you say it's that way?" he said, intentionally pointing in the opposite direction.

"No, that way," I said, pointing in the correct direction.

"Ohhh. So lemme get this straight once again. I go down this street, turn left...Well, do you mind just walking with me a little of the ways. You know, just so I know where I'm going."

"No," I said, not because I feared the stranger; I didn't want Grandma Anita to come looking for me and couldn't find me.

Before I could turn away, he grabbed my arm and pulled out a knife.

"I'll slice your throat if you yell," he said, his lips pressed tightly against my right temple.

He dragged me backwards to a house located behind the nearby hospital parking lot.

"Please....please. I just learned how to skate," I pleaded as the wheels of my skates screeched against the pavement.

When he felt we were out of view, he let go his grip, dropping me into the tall, prickly weeds. Before I could muster a word out of my mouth or even attempt to scream, he socked me right in the throat.

"I said, don't say a word," he warned, now straddling my frail frame.

The weeds were way too tall for anyone to this man committing this egregious crime against me. So unless I outright disobeyed his former commands to shut up, he was definitely going to have his way with me.

"Yeah, just like I like it," he said, fondling me through my clothes.

The flight–fight mechanism kicked in. I started kicking and trying to use force to throw him off me. "Get off me! Get off me!"

He pressed my face, sideways to the ground. Although he no longer had the knife in his hand, he threatened to use it once again. "I'll slice your throat, little gal. You better shut the hell up," he said in a firm tone.

I stopped struggling, but tears began to roll down my cheeks.

Just as with Grandma Anita, my tears meant nothing. He pulled my pants down and ripped my thin underwear. With his legs, he forced my legs apart, holding my slim wrists with one hand. He tore my shirt off with his free hand, rendering me completely naked. He stopped for a moment. He glared into my eyes as if he was having consensual sex with a consenting adult.

"Now that's a good girl. All I wanted was directions," he added as he thrust his manhood in my vagina. I closed my eyes. If death could just have taken me away in that moment, it would have been a fair exchange. My body rocked back and forth, back and forth for what seemed like an eternity. Then, he let out a howl that sounded like a werewolf, and he stopped moving.

With my eyes still closed, I curled up into a ball.

"Hey, hey—" he yelled.

I opened my eyes.

"Get up."

I squirmed on the ground until I could muster up enough strength so stand. I pulled my pants back up. He had used such force to pull them down that he popped the buttons on the waistband.

"Stand over there," he said, pointing to a nearby tree.

I leaned against a nearby tree and watched him pull his pants back up, straighten up his disheveled hair, and wipe the sweat from his face.

"I want to you stand there and count to a thousand before you come outta here. You hear me?"

I nodded. But I don't think I bothered to count at all. I was so scared for many reasons, including the fact that I was late getting around the block and I had used the bathroom in my pants. There was another set of consequences attached to both of these things. But I tucked my shirt in my pants as neatly as I could, wiped my face, adjusted my skates, and made my way back home, stopping at points in between due to the throbbing and burning sensation between my legs.

The family was still out on the front porch laughing and talking when I skated up to the porch. A bit disheveled, I sat down on the bottom step and started unloosening my skates. Grandma Anita must have been a semi-good mood because she didn't light in on me for being late.

I beckoned for Grandma Anita to follow me into the house.

"Grandma, I need to talk to you," I said, softly.

"Girl, can't you see I'm out here talking to grown-ups?" she said, getting up from her seat all the while.

I stood silent. I knew it was going to be hard enough telling Grandma Anita in private what had just happened, let alone, telling her in front of the whole clan.

As I walked up the porch stairs, tears filled my eyes.

Having noticed my watering eyes, Grandma Anita crossed over in front of me and opened the front door. "Now, what is it?" she said, closing the door behind her.

I recalled the entire ordeal, now crying inconsolably. Grandma Anita stood still. She was devoid of any emotion or concern. I wondered if she'd heard me. The silence was creepy. Finally, she spoke.

"Girl, why you makin' up stories like that? Did you fall down? Is that what happened? You fell down and hurt yourself down there, didn't you?"

"ANITA! I screamed! A man touched my private parts!"

I don't know what stunned me more—the fact that I'd had the gall to yell and call Grandma Anita by her first name, or that, in the midst of all my theatrics, she raised her backhand smacked me, causing me to fall backwards.

"Shut your godda*n mouth! Nothin' happened to you. You weren't doing nuthin' but out there being fast!" she said. "Get upstairs, you dirty ole heifer!"

She came upstairs to my room a few minutes later.

"Here," she said, throwing a bath towel at me.

I picked the towel up and slid my bottom to the edge of the bed. The burning and throbbing had intensified.

"Let's hit the bathroom," she said. I came to fully understand on this day that for Grandma Anita, taking a bath symbolized ridding yourself of the dirt and guilt. At some point while she was scrubbing my back, I brought the subject back up.

"What's going to happen to that man?"

"What man? Dammit, shut up! You need to stop all this lying you're doing, gal! If that man is out there, he's probably long gone by now. So don't you go telling this wild story to anybody else, ya hear me? You do, and I'mma do more than scrub your little ass!"

Although gravely distraught and confused, I nodded. I didn't understand why Grandma Anita didn't believe me, or better yet, why she refused to. Nevertheless, I remained clear on one thing—Grandma Anita wasn't to be crossed. If she instructed me not to say anything to anybody, I knew I couldn't tell a soul, not even Grand-dad Carlos, who was going to be home shortly. He had promised to take me to our favorite spot—Buffalo International Airport.

∞ ∞ ∞ ∞

"Tiffer, is you ready baby?" Granddad asked as soon as he walked in that afternoon.

I put on my happy face. His voice was all I needed to hear to make me come running and bring to my shattered soul, some solace. Hanging Granddad Carlos was my great escape. I jumped in his arms and gave him a big hug. When he put me down, I dug deep in his pockets for his quarters like I always did. I tried hard to be normal and happy. Grandma Anita stood behind him, giving me "the eye", as if to remind me to keep my lips sealed. I smiled at Granddad Carlos and ran out the front door, down the steps, and hopped into his Cadillac.

As always, we headed to the hot dog and milkshake stands and then went back to sit in his 1981 Cadillac to watch the airplanes take off. We pretended that the airplanes were magic carpets en route to faraway lands, and for that moment in time, I felt safe. For a brief moment, everything was okay. To me, this was what love and peace felt like—not having to look over my shoulder for fear of a fist or stretched hand coming at me. Neither did I have to walk on eggshells, fearful that someone would find fault in my washing the dishes, folding clothes, or vacuuming the carpet.

But as much as I enjoyed moments like this, I was always haunted by the thought that I was going to be short lived. Sooner or later, we were going to head back to 920 Lafayette. So I just decided to enjoy it for what it was—temporary pleasure.

After the sunset, Granddad Carlos started his car up. "You know we have to head on back before your grandma goes into a tizzy."

I nodded.

"If Granddad could have his way, we'd get on one of these here planes and go on us a little vacation. Just me and you."

I smiled. That made me feel special.

Granddad patted me on my leg. "I have a feeling you're going to fly in many airplanes one day. You're going to be someone famous."

Every seven-year old wants to be famous. But this declaration meant something different to me—Granddad Carlos's words revved up something in my soul.

Raising Cain When She is "Able"

I was never a daughter ...
Only born a woman
Ahead of my time, right on schedule
Depleted of a childhood
Yet, seasoned like Lawry's
With the discernment to
Recognize poultry from beef
Plastic from rubber
Truth from fallacy
Fiction from reality

Hated by the assigned Cain's
In my life, because they knew
That my birth symbolized
The end of an era and
Just how ABLE I would become...
They knew the battle to destroy
The Generational Curse
On our dysfunctional lineage
Was by me already won
So thank you for wounding me
Leaving me for dead
For my blood saturated the soil

And cried out
From your inflicted lacerations
By which I bled...

You see
This isn't who my father created me to be
He has too much invested
For me to be found living beneath my
dignity
Compromising my character
Prostituting my gift
Embracing mediocrity, instead...
I became addicted to accountability
For it brought out the best in me

You see, I understand "CAIN"
While many don't understand they're
"ABLE"
To possess the ability to be
Powerful...
With one's unprecedented capacity...
Untouchable physicality...
In-depth mentality...
Undeniable spiritually...

Intellectually sound...
Aptitude above ground...
Gifted to perform in an arena

Where many will never be found

While behind the curtains
There is an enemy crouching
Knowing of my ABLE-ity
Having had a backstage pass to my
destiny
Attempting to lower my resistance....
Abort my tranquility

For they know that
If they can't raise CAIN
They'd be forced to witness to
The birth of ABLE
So there I was, live in living color
Suffocating in my own sovereignty
Infected with the problem of...
Thinking I can do it by myself
Not knowing when you're ABLE
You need special care
I often look up and see
That there is no one there

To protect my natural self sufficiency
For my ABLE-ty renders me
Independent but too trusting
Venerable but vulnerable
Focused and yet slightly distracted

Gifted and sometimes gullible
Elevated to the state of loneliness
Maintaining
Unbothered
Unaffected

While bouncing back UP
Taking that licking and keep on ticking
Grounded not by sanity
But by my ability
Unlike regular people
Leaving
those in observation
Fascinated yet mistakenly
Thinking
That just because she got
back up from the dirt
Meant that I wasn't hurt

Oh...
But...
CAIN where is your sister
She has ABLE-ty
Who's looking out for her?
In the room full of ABLE people
With NO one in the corner
Who will protect he gift
Just watch her

Pour, pour and pour
Elevate and support
Push
Cover
Pray
Those who drain
Know not her name
Whose
Pouring into her
Covering her
Praying for her
Who is in her corner?

Wait
Cause I'm ABLE
Yet so tired
That I've reached a level of fatigue
Those 12 hours of sleep can compete
Passion filled
Longing for interdependency
Filled with an innate expectancy
To stand strong
Daily telling my tears
Don't you dare fall...
Don't you dare fall...
Out of my eyes
Keep it together
This storm you must weather

 I know my ability
Understand the scrutiny
The weight of my destiny
Halting everything
Understanding that
I am the ABLE, favored to keep the flock
While CAIN worked a cursed soil
Which his birthright isn't kept
I've relegated to the fact
That Favor carries you where
Experience need not to
Truth is I know now that
I need you and
It's time to STOP RAISING Cain
Because of my birthright

I was born ABLE...

She Speaks

CHAPTER FOUR

Thrown into the Pit

A s in the life of Joseph, imagine having your own family beat you, throw you into a pit and leave you to die. Just when you thought, they had a change of heart, you discover they come back only to sell you into slavery. Have you lost heart? Would you sit there and nurse resentment? Joseph didn't! Do you have the courage and faith it takes to still do great things despite the bad things that others have done to you? Stay with me, the journey continues.

∞ ∞ ∞ ∞

January 7, 1984, was a cold day in Buffalo, both literally and figuratively. The call came in about 4:30 pm. Granddad Carlos told Grandma Anita that he had been having chest pains since early that morning.

Grandma Anita might have acted like to could take or leave Granddad, but after his call to her that afternoon, I saw a different side of Grandma Anita surface—she was actually scared. Sweat pebbles broke out all over her face.

She licked her lips. "Umm....go straight on over to Buffalo General, and I'll meet you there," she said, pacing back and forth in the kitchen.

I don't even think she gave Granddad Carlos the opportunity to respond because she slammed the phone down on the receiver so fast and rushed upstairs. I followed, a bit out of curiosity but more out of fear and anxiety.

"Who was that, grandma?" I said, watching change her clothes.

"Nobody, Tiff...nobody," she said, putting on her wig and adjusting it to fit her liking.

I couldn't resist the burning quest to ask if something was wrong with Granddad Carlos. She was well aware that Granddad and I had a special bond, and word of him falling ill would have crushed my heart.

"Is it granddad?" I asked anyway.

"Tiff, it's nobody. I'll be right back." She grabbed her raggedy black purse and whisked past me and down the stairs. I ran down right behind her.

"Lock this door behind me, and don't you open it for no one. You and Garry watch TV in the living room until I get back, you hear?"

I nodded and closed and locked the door as instructed.

∞ ∞ ∞ ∞

By the time Granddad Carlos arrived at Buffalo General, he was having a full-fledged stroke. The news had traveled around, and several of our family members had gathered at the hospital. While still waiting for news on Granddad Carlos's improvement, he suffered a massive heart attack. The combination of both the stroke and the heart attack had done too much damage to his vital organs, and he died.

Having already sensed that the call was about Granddad Carlos, I didn't need any further explanation from Grandma Anita when she and Aunt Denise came back to the house later on that night. Garry had fallen asleep in the living room, and Grandma Anita walked right past him sprawled out over the floor and went upstairs to her bedroom. She didn't say two words to me.

"What's wrong, Aunt Denise?" I said, turning to look at her. Her eyes were red and her eyelids puffy.

"Daddy died tonight," she said in a soft whisper.

Everything went black for a moment. The sound of the TV seemed to fade into the abyss. My knees began to buckle. Granddad Carlos—my savior, my rock, my best friend—had left me. All I could think of was that my world had come crashing down. I couldn't imagine my life without him.

Granddad Carlos's wake was held on January 12, 1984, in the formal dining room of our house. Everyone wore black and bore solemn faces. Per Grandma Anita, kids weren't allowed to attend, grandchildren or not. She instructed my older cousin, Marie, to give the kids a warm shot of Brandy and put us all to bed.

I might not have been permitted to attend the "formal" service for Granddad Carlos, but what I experienced that night was a far better experience. Somehow that Brandy hadn't done what it was intended to do, which was to put me to sleep. I just couldn't wind my emotions down enough to go to sleep either. I hadn't laid eyes on Granddad for five consecutive days, and I was missing him terribly.

I lay there staring at the ceiling, then at the wall. Suddenly, I saw a reflection. It was a silhouette of a man with wings. My eyes following the silhouette as it moved across the wall and waved as if it were saying good-bye. I sat upright. I was convinced that the silhouette was Granddad Carlos paying me a special visit to say good-bye.

Marie came in the room a few minutes later to check on us.

"I just saw granddad," I blurted out.

Believing it to be the result of the Brandy she had given me, she smiled. "Where?" "Over there," I said, pointing to the wall.

She looked over at the wall, looked out of the window, and then closed the curtains. "Go to sleep," she said, kissing me on the forehead.

∞ ∞ ∞ ∞

920 Lafayette (not that any day did) didn't feel right the next day. Although Granddad Carlos was gone physically, emotionally he was right by my side. The ground was frozen solid and Granddad Carlos couldn't be buried until sometime in the spring, when the ground thawed and his grave could be dug.

I saw Grandma Anita cry for the first time the next morning after Granddad Carlos died. Strangely enough, I could feel her pain. Thinking that Grandma Anita had softened up a bit, I grabbed my box of Crayola crayons and sat in the corner of her bedroom. I found myself sketching pictures of all the things that made me happy. Drawing was the only way I could express the depth of my feelings and how much I missed Granddad Carlos. After all, there was no one else to talk to, considering that conversation wasn't the norm with me in this house. As I was coloring in the flowers on my Picasso of sorts, Grandma Anita walked in. I erred in thinking that Granddad Carlos's death had softened her somewhat. Before I knew it, she snatched me up by my collar so fast, that my head was literally spinning. I dropped the crayons I held in my hands.

"Ain't nobody here to save your ass now!" she taunted as she dragged me out of the room. I clutched the teddy bear that Granddad had given me, which I had brought in the room with me.

"You think you're so f**kin' special 'cause he loved you more than he loved me? I don't think so! If he hadn't found your little ass, you'd be out there right alongside him!" Grandma Anita continued with her ranting speech as she pulled me down the stairs, causing me to collect several splinters and abrasions on my face, arms and legs.

I remember coming to an abrupt stop at the bottom of the stairs on the cold concrete floor of the basement. Even though it was still daylight outside, the basement was dark. It always stayed that way. The basement was not insulated or finished, so it was cold. I looked around at what would be my bedroom, living room, kitchen, and bathroom for the next few days. This type of punishment was a "has been". I suffered through it before.

A small puddle sat in the corner, which came from the sewer. The water was mixed with the lye that had been placed on the floor during one of the many floods. Together, they created a horrible stench. Through the screen of the window, I could see my dog, Sonny. I stared out at him as the hours passed, wishing I could be where he was instead of being locked up in the basement. Days had passed and I remained in the basement with no food, no personal contact, no school, no anything. I could only hear footsteps above my head.

∞ ∞ ∞ ∞

When I returned to school after about a week, long enough to allow the bumps and bruises to disappear, I remained quiet. Administration and staff were aware that my grandfather had passed, so they sort of just thought that my week-long absence was related to bereavement.

I was abnormally quiet and reserved, however, and that's because Grandma Anita had warned to "keep the white man outta our business." Her words vibrated through my bones, it seemed. On my way back to class from the lavatory, Sister Peggy stopped me.

"Hi, Tiffany."

I waved.

"We missed you," she said, walking up to me.

I looked down. Although I was sure of what "not" to say, I wasn't so sure of just what I could say.

"Your hair is very pretty," she continued, attempting to touch my ponytail.

I moved my head back.

"Sorry. Did I do something wrong," she said, taken aback by my nonverbal response.

I didn't answer.

"Tell me something, Tiffany," she said, crouching down to become eye level with me. "Where's your mother?" she blurted out.

"Umm...my mom ran away when I was little," I offered, thinking I hadn't offered too much information.

Sister Peggy swallowed hard. When I look back in hindsight, I believe I provided her with a piece of the puzzle that she had been trying to figure out. From that moment on, until I left D.E.C., Sister Peggy and I enjoyed a special bond. She took me under her wing, so to speak.

"Well, go on back to class," Sister Peggy said as she wrapped her long arms around me and gave me a warm embrace. I flinched with pain. If she had only taken the time to look under my long sleeves and turtlenecks, she would have seen the bruises that had been inflicted upon me. She would have seen the scabs that were forming from the cuts the extension cord had made. She could have possibly put an end to the abuse. But I never spoke on the abuse, she never looked, and the physical and emotional scars were never discovered. In reality, I wanted to scream out *HELP ME!* But I simply couldn't. In the face of freedom, I was too committed to bondage and lost for words. When I could have possibly ended the madness, I became clammy and mute. I didn't trust anyone, considering my own flesh and blood had violated me for so long. I lived everyday with an overwhelming amount of guilt on my shoulders, believing the neglect, abuse, rape and the years of endless rejection were because of my doing. Even more so, I feared my Grandma Anita's reaction had the police come knocking on her door. She was the master of manipulation, and combined with an element of the unknown, I was compelled to remain silent. The harsh reality was that I had grown accustomed to my dysfunctional life, and for the sake of family, I sincerely held on to the notion that silence was my only option. I lived day after day feeling powerless because I had long learned from tangible examples that speaking out was a disease that had no cure—it was terminal.

∞ ∞ ∞ ∞

By the following school year, the bond between Sister Peggy and me had grown even tighter. She was always buying me small gifts. Right before Christmas that year, she gave me a garbage bag full of toys. She drove me home from school because the bag was too heavy for me to carry on the bus. Excited, I was. However, it was short lived, like many of my other happier days. Grandma Anita did not allow me to keep the gifts.

"We don't accept handouts," Grandma Anita said, throwing the bag into the dumpster in our backyard.

I never saw Sister Peggy again. After winter break that year, Grandma Anita withdrew me from D.E.C. and enrolled me in Public School 56, on Buffalo's west side.

∞ ∞ ∞ ∞

School continued to be my greatest place of escape, allowing me to get away from the hate and abuse, even just for a little while. But now, being in public school and away from the protection of the Sisters, I slowly became a different person.

During one of my many periods of starvation, I resorted to doing what my Aunt Denise had taught me to do best—steal. Recycling was a fad at that time, so to speak, and people would bag up their cans and take them over to Bell's to get money. I walk over to Bell's and wait behind the parked cars. As soon as the store clerks turned their heads and walked away, I would grab a bag of cans and run home as fast as I could. At home, I would take the cans out of one bag, put them in another one, and return them to another grocery store to collect money for them.

This particular heist became ritualistic for me. But like most repeat offenders, it was only a matter of time before I got caught. One day in the spring, I cut morning classes on my quest to get money. I did my morning dirt with the soda cans and stopped at Wendy's en route to school, picking up some burgers for me and my classmates before checking into school. Feeling invincible, I took the food into the school, and, while trying to sneak into my afternoon classes, I was spotted by the school principal, Mr. Robinson.

"Tiffany Duson!" he yelled, looking at me and then the Wendy's bag.

I took off running, bolting through a set of doors that led to the social studies corridor. I could hear the sound of feet chasing behind me. I picked up my pace.

"Ooooohhh sh*tttttt!" Principal Robinson shrieked.

I stopped and turned around. The principal was lying in the hallway, holding his left ankle with both hands. I didn't bother trying to help him. Instead, I turned back around to head to class. But before take a step, I was snatched up by the hall monitor and taken to the principal's office. Protocol was a call to Grandma Anita and suspension. I knew I was in for a thrashing. The worst part of it was the wait.

When I got home, I was immediately ordered to the basement and instructed to wait. This time, however, I refused to sit idly, waiting to be brutalized. *Just as I had managed to avert the principal's intended punishment, I could avert Grandma Anita's,* I thought.

I knew the window in the fecal-spattered bathroom was just big enough for me to slither my way through. The basement was the storage hub of our house, everything you can from bikes, old clothes, trash, books and toys was stored in it. This was the one area of the house that the "neat freak" allowed to fall into despair. I just needed to find something to stand up on to reach the window. So I piled up some boxes and bags, opened the screen window, and pushed the screen out. Sonny was asleep in his doghouse. I slid through the window and literally ran for my life.

I darted through the backyards of several of our neighbors. While I had no clue where I was going, I kept running and didn't look back once. My immediate objective was simply to get as far away from 920 Lafayette as I physically could. My spirit felt like that of the slaves that Harriet Tubman transported through the Underground Railroad—my mindset was, if I could just make it to the other side of the unknown, I'd be okay.

After sometime, I finally slowed down and started walking, and I kept walking until I ended up in Elmwood. This was the nicer part of town. I stopped at a payphone to find a phonebook. Ironically, there was an advertisement for runaways on the first page. It listed an 800-number, so I dialed it. The lady on the other end of the telephone gave me details about the safe house, including its confidentiality policy, as well as the address. I hung up the payphone and took a deep breath. My journey into independence had begun.

∞ ∞ ∞ ∞

After she signed me in, the intake counselor, a white woman who looked to be in her mid-to-late sixties, went over the house rules and advised me on the particulars of what was called a forty-eight-hour "cooling off period". Essentially, it meant that they provided runaways forty-eight hours of anonymity before mapping out a plan for the runaway. Upon learning this information, I quickly agreed to the rules. But as with most things, there was a caveat—if the police came to the residence for any reason, including if they were sent by parents searching for their missing children, I could be asked to leave. I had some reserve, but in that moment, returning to 920 Lafayette Street was out of the question.

"There's tons of food, cable television, books, and a counselor to talk to if you needed one," she said, handing me some literature.

I clicked with a group of girls in the home on the first day. The three of them shared with me their stories as to why they had run away—two of the girls had run away after fighting with their parents, and the third girl had been repeatedly molested by her father and finally left because she was tired of keeping the secret. I related easily to all three of the girls because we all had the same thing in common—we were afraid of returning to our places of torment.

As the days progressed, I learned that these girls were not only "victims", they were also professional thieves! Since my arrival, I had witnessed them devise and implement daily schemes involving shoplifting, robbery, and any other hustle that would bring them money. It was all about survival of the fittest. I was enjoying my newfound independence and simply wanted to fit in. One day, the girls planned to go shopping downtown and asked me if I wanted to come. With full knowledge that none of us had any money, I agreed anyway. What the girls referred to as shopping was actually boosting. I had some initial reservation, but after contemplating upping my fashion in clothes and shoes, I was all game.

The girls made it a point to try to "show me the ropes" before we officially headed out on our heist.

"You need a pair of sweats," Deneen said, looking me over to guestimate my size.

"I don't have any," I said, looking down at the faded denim pants I was wearing. Grandma Anita never bought me real clothes. She'd given me clothes of Cousin Garry's to wear, and I got hand-me-downs from the Goodwill or what other kids passed on to me. So I was down to get myself something decent and nice for once.

"Don't worry. I got you. I have a pair of sweats with pockets you can wear," Deneen replied.

That was it. I had volunteered to hit my first lick with my clique. So with the vouchers given to us, we took the bus to AMA's, which was like the Macy's of the 80s. The girls knew the layout very well. The store had three floors and three exit areas. We walked with our big coats and book bags, and loose clothes and rushed over to the junior's section. We knew we had to be fast and quick. We grabbed a few outfits and headed straight to the dressing room. The trick was to dress in as many clothes as you could without looking suspicious. Whatever you couldn't put on, had to be stuffed into the book bag.

"Let's meet up across the street at Woolworth's," Deneen whispered as we passed the dressing room attendant.

A lump formed in my throat and a ball in my stomach as I slowly walked into my assigned dressing room stall. If I got caught, it would mean going back to Grandma Anita's. I didn't even think about the fact that I could be arrested for stealing, or anything else, for that matter. I only thought about getting taken back to Grandma Anita's house and being beaten. *That, in and of itself, would be worse than any punishment the "white man" could ever give me.*

But I was already in knee deep, so I padded myself with four outfits, left a few on the hangers in the stall as a prop, and excited the stall.

"How did you make out?" the attendant asked.

"I think I'm going to get this," I said, holding up a red and grey two-piece, pants outfit. I barely made eye contact with the attendant, but I distinctly remembered she said had what sounded like a Caribbean accent.

I threw the two-piece pants outfit on top of a rack on my way out of the store and ran across the street to our meeting ground. They had already boosted earrings and other accessories. They were laughing and joking while I, on the other hand, was sick to my stomach with fright and simply wanted some food. I had a few dollars in my pockets from the money I'd gotten for the cans a couple days back, so I ran upstairs with my bags to Burger King and got a burger and soda. The girls came upstairs and sat with me. Once I got some food in me I started to feel better and relaxed. We sat there a while and bragged about how bad we were, and the fact that we had not been caught.

A few hours later, we returned to the house and spread the stolen goods on the bed. I was happy to finally have something clean and new to wear. I jumped in the shower, brushed my teeth, and got dressed in my new digs. I was elated, on a high. I had never felt so free in my life. It almost matched the feeling I used to get from hanging out with Granddad Carlos. It had been two months since his death, and I missed him sorely. I couldn't help but think that if he hadn't died, I wouldn't have been in the present circumstance. But the reality was he was gone for good.

After we'd tried on this and that, and oohed and ahhed over our stolen goods, we ventured into our separate rooms and routines. I went downstairs to watch television and was interrupted by one of the counselors, Mrs. Glenn, I believe was her name.

"How's it going?" she asked, taking a seat next to me.

"Good. I'm doing good," I said, shifting my posture to make extra room for Mrs. Glenn, who was obese.

"I'm glad to hear that. We have to check in with all of our girls after a period of time."

"Okay," I said, in a somewhat ambivalent manner, sensing she had some bad news to share.

"Would be interested in speaking with one of our social workers so that they can further evaluate you to determine your eligibility to continue in the program?"

That's when I broke down. "I don't want to go home," I sobbed. Since I hadn't been going to school, I wasn't able to stay at the shelter. I mean, it too, had its own set of unique rules.

"All the girls that stay here are only allowed to do so if they attend school on a daily basis," Mrs. Glenn said, reaching over to pull Kleenex out of the box on the end table next to the love seat we were sitting on.

"But I'm on suspension," I said between sobs. "The only way I can get back into school is if my grandmother comes in and talks to the teacher." I pleaded with her with my eyes. There was no way I wanted to go back to Grandma Anita's house. Just the few days of freedom that I'd had were better than any so-called good day in that house. But my pleas meant nothing. Mrs. Glenn just shook her head.

"I'm sorry. If you're not in school you can't stay here. You should really think about going home. Your forty-eight hours are almost up."

I nodded my head, but I didn't say a word. I knew that I had to leave the house, but I was certain that 'home'—Grandma Anita's house—was not where I was going.

On that Thursday morning, I packed my few bags. I was scared and very sad to say good-bye to my new-found friends. I felt like I belonged there. For once, I felt as if there were others in my same situation that had made their way out. I left as much as I could behind

because I had no idea where I was going, and I needed to have as little as possible so as not to be weighed
down in the event that I had to run. The weather had
grown colder, and I was freezing. But with very few
options, I walked and walked until my feet got tired.
By the end of the day, I was deep in the west side
of Buffalo, which was surrounded by town homes
and vintage buildings that were much nicer than the
ones in my old neighborhood. I immediately recognized
it as a "white people area" that I had only daydreamed
about. With my smarts, wits, charm, and street know-
how, I knew I would have no problem blending in with
the community.

The next day, I disguised myself as a student,
dressed in a gray-hooded sweatshirt, with thermal
underwear beneath, a brown, winter beanie, blue jeans,
and high-top sneakers. I had no problem fitting it. I followed the neighborhood kids to school. I hung out in the
bathroom during school session and hid in stalls when
students came in between classes and during lunchtime.
I even caught up on some much needed sleep. I stayed
in there all day until the last bell rang. This shenani-
gan worked for three days, and then I had to move on.
I was worried someone would catch on to me, and
I didn't want to risk the chances of being caught.

By the following Saturday, just a few days into
my newest journey, I was hungry and cold. I couldn't
find quite enough of scraps in the garbage to munch

on. The cold, March weather made things even more complicated. But that's when I devised a new scheme. I would sit on the stairs of people's homes. When they would approach me on their way home, I'd tell them that I was lost, hungry, and needed to use their phones. I'd always make sure to use the soap in the bathrooms of fast food restaurants to wash my face so I looked clean. The unassuming victims would invite me into their homes, and when they would disappear for a few moments, be it was to use the bathroom, retrieve the telephone for me, or get some food to put in my stomach, I'd make my move. For some reason, the women I encountered seemed to have had a habit of dropping their purses and keys on the table the moment they walked in. That's when I would go in for the kill and snatch their wallet. When they would come back into the room, I'd pretend to make a call but tell the friendly stranger that I couldn't get through because of a busy signal. Then, I'd excuse myself. I managed to get away without getting caught on each of the three occasions that I pulled this particular scam. So I had a few dollars to get me by for a couple of days.

By the following Tuesday, I had come down with a cold. Despite feeling that staying gone was better than being home, I did wonder whether anyone was concerned about my whereabouts. I decided to call home and let Grandma Anita know that I was okay. I used a payphone across the street from laundromat in Elmwood. Grandma Anita answered.

"Grandma Anita? It's me. I just wanted to call and say that I'm okay. I'm eating, and I'm safe." Having said all that I'd intended to say, I was ready to hang up, but Grandma Anita wouldn't let it go that easily.

"Where are you?"

"I'm not going to say," I answered nervously.

"You better get your ass back here. I've already called the police on you. You're gonna come back here either with or without them. I'd rather you bring your tail back without them—keep them folks out my business."

I didn't say anything. She sounded calm enough, but I knew that there was another side that was just waiting until she got her hands on me. As cold as I was, and as much as I wanted to be somewhere warm and safe, I knew that being with her *wasn't* that place.

"I'll tell you what," she continued. "If you don't bring your ass home, and those white mother******s show up on my doorstep, I'm gonna tell them to keep your ass. Now bring your goddamn ass home!"

"Promise you won't hit me?" I asked hopefully.

"Who the f**k do you think you are?" she yelled. "Is that what you been telling them white folks? I'm a give them something to talk about—don't you worry about me. Bring your ass home or don't call this goddamn house again!"

She didn't wait for me to say anything else. She just slammed down the receiver. I was scared, running out of money and places to hide. The snow was still on the ground, and I needed a bath and new clothes. I decided the best thing for me to do was to go home. Trekked my way back home.

I stood at the bottom of the concrete steps. It was just about five or six stairs up, but seemed like twenty stairs in front of me. Walking up and pressing the doorbell was essentially volunteering for added abuse and suffering. But the cold Buffalo weather and its mean streets, didn't offer safety and comfort either. I took the first step.

"Suffa-Ring"

The bell rings and the fight is on
But so one-sided...so brutal...
just so...so...damning
Before I'm at an age where I can
comprehend
Before I can cultivate the strength
to begin
I am hit with gladiator style blows that
rock me to my core
Teeth and blood seep from my soul...
this caged bird sings no more
I never had a training class...never signed
up for this bout
But pain led the way to education...
un-graded tests line this route
I pray for the bell...for a break...for the
Ref to end it
For someone with a bullet...and a willing
gun to send it

There are no rounds to this fight...I am
just boxed in
And I glance at the first few rows of the
crowd...and wonder
Why are they covered with plastic
sheets?

And then his fist connects with my
mouth...and plastic meets my teeth
But there is something carnal that lies
within mankind
A place that the mind can't go...
but the body knows
Where imminent death raises
its ugly head
And it is then that all limbs act
without regard
For life knows how to fight for itself
That next breath is the goal...not family,
fame or wealth

Ahhh...that point in life brought me
clarity I didn't know existed
And strength I didn't know was
stored away
Gave me an edge that I never imagined
that I had
That cling to hold onto life...and just STAY
Last thru it
Make it past
Excuse my language...but I had to hold
the f**k on
Sorry to sensitive ears...exposed
to a lifelong fight with wrong

All my sorrow caused me to reject the
willingness to die
And I outlasted my enemies...but not
because I tried
I simply held on and refused to give in
Smiled at the Ref...until he too joined in
I wore out all that dared to wrap hands
around my throat
Ignored shameful stares...and the crowd
change of note
The worst that came at me...the hideous
things that people give
But I got the best revenge and justice
imaginable...still here, still Live

CHAPTER FIVE

Attempted Murder

The summer of 1985 had arrived. The temperature outside soared above eighty degrees and was muggy. It was the kind of weather where you couldn't wait to get home, strip down, and put on those new linen shorts that you got at the mall. With my book bag somewhere deep in the closet, like the years past, preparing for the first day of school was the last thing on my mind. All I really was trying to do was get out that front door in a hurry. I can remember rushing down the stairs and putting on my sneakers in an attempt to get out of the house.

"Where do you think you're going?" Grandma Anita asked, stopping me at the bottom of the stairs. "Who told you that you could go anywhere? Since when did you start socializing? Don't you have homework? What did you do today?" she continued, asking a slew of questions and hoping to trip me up with one of them.

"I'm going to Tiffany's, remember? You said I could. I have two book reports due, but they're not due until September—school's out," I said, trying to make sure I answered all of her questions.

My responses seemed to appease her. She stepped back, and I skirted by her and darted outside before she had a chance to change her mind. I didn't get moments like this too often, so I definitely wanted to take advantage of it. I knew I'd be forced to start in on school work soon enough.

By mid-July, I began to focus on my book reports. One of the books I chose was *I Know Why the Caged Bird Sings* by Maya Angelou. I fell in love with poetry that summer and this would later become one of my favorite books, next to anything written by Randall Robinson.

The day I was nearing the completion of the first book report, I noticed that new neighbors were moving in next door. It appeared to be a single woman and a little boy who I presumed to be her son. He looked to be about six- or seven-years old. I took the liberty of welcoming them to the neighborhood.

"Hi," I said to the boy when his mother went into the house.

"Hi," he responded with a smile.

"How old are you? Where are you from?" I asked, repeating Grandma Anita's antic of asking several questions at once.

Before the boy could speak, Grandma Anita interrupted. "Tiffany, who are you talking to? Get your ass in this house!"

As ordered, I went in the house.

"I can't leave you for two seconds!" Grandma Anita taunted coming toward me. "You're out there being a little fast-ass. Your momma was a tramp, and you itching to be just like her, I see."

"I was just saying hello," I said, defending my honest action.

Her backhand came at me like something out of The Matrix. I gasped and clutched my right hand over my right cheek.

"Say one more thing, and see if you're not swallowing teeth," she hissed before turning her back toward me.

The sound of her voice brought me back to reality— I was living with a monster. But I was so busy reveling in my own hurt and pain that I didn't initially see what Grandma Anita was doing. When she turned around brandishing a six-inch butcher knife. To say that I was shocked is an understatement.

"Since you've got so much mouth, maybe you want to see how your momma felt when she got her throat slit. Is that what you want? I may not have brought you in this world, but I have no problem taking you out!" she continued, swaying the knife back and forth in front of my eyes.

"No, I don't want to be like my momma!" I screamed between sobs, pleading with her not to hit me, not to cut me.

"You always around here thinking you're special or something. Should have been you that died instead of your granddad. But then he always loved your little ass more than he loved me anyhow. That's what killed him—always worrying about you. *You* killed him!"

The venom in her words stung me harder than anything. She waved the knife back and forth in the air as she continued to rant. Before I could move back far enough, she lunged at me, toward my heart. I held my hands up in an attempt to block the knife from going into my chest. Blood oozed from my left arm. The stinging pain followed.

Grandma Anita's eyes widened. Either she was shocked over how far she had actually gone or she was shocked that she hadn't been successful in stabbing me in the heart. With force, she pulled the knife out, and with it, a chunk of my flesh.

I fell to my knees, clenched my right hand over the wound and hollered out in intense pain. Blood gushed out, soaking my clothes and forming a puddle on the floor. I remember looking at Grandma Anita—she had a faraway look in her eyes, as if she weren't even in the room. It seemed like several minutes had passed before she snapped out of her trance. In that moment, she ran to the kitchen and brought back a concoction that consisted of baking soda, peroxide, and talcum powder. First, she bathed my arm in peroxide. Next, she poured alcohol into the wound. Then, she caked my arm with the homemade paste concoction and placed some toilet tissue over it.

Once she was sure that she'd successfully stopped the bleeding and had the wound all cleaned up, she sent me to my room. I was about mid-way up the stairs when she called me back.

"Anyone asks you what happened, you tell 'em that you fell on a piece of glass, you hear me?"

I gave her the obligatory nod. The cover up speech was nothing new. I was used to it by now. Most of the time, Grandma Anita limited her abuse to areas that could be concealed by long sleeves or pants legs. She made sure to steer clear of my face, not leaving any visible marks for the public eye. I usually had so many bruises on my body that I rarely wore anything short. In fact, I'm not even sure if I owned anything short. I didn't see where this incident would be any different, but what she said next let me know how different this really was.

"Mess around and say something other than what I just told you, and I'll be sure to finish what I started."

I believed that Grandma Anita meant it and would follow through on the threat. After all, she had just tried to ram a six-inch steak knife through my heart.

I went upstairs with the weight of her threat on my heart. I truly felt like a prisoner who had been inside a cell for ten years. I felt a sudden urge to tell everyone my pain. I wanted to break out—defy her and pick up the phone and call the police. Granddad Carlos was now only a figment in my dreams, and there was no one else to save me. But my dilemma was, *where do you go when you're only nine years old?*

∞ ∞ ∞ ∞

With no allies, I felt as if I were going to die in that house, and deep down the thought horrified me. It, alone, was enough to solidify my decision to run away again. This time, though, I made up my mind that come hell or high water, I was not coming back. Ironically, however, was the fact that once I made the decision, I found myself constantly struggling to cope with the notion of abandoning Grandma Anita. Even though she treated me horribly, I loved her a great deal—at least in the twisted way that I'd grown to view love. Looking back, I'd have to equate the feelings I felt then to that of a woman suffering from battered woman's syndrome. I had followed in the footsteps of the Duson family women—we struggled with healing our personal wounds and managed to keep our battle scars hidden from everyone else's view. Internally, we wrestled with the notion of abuse as acceptable and common. At some point, I was able to connect the dots and put the pieces to a complex puzzle together, piece by piece. I knew then that I wanted something different, something better.

Close enough to spit

I hate you and I cannot remember why
But it seethes in me...breathes in me
The good parts of you that I see...I am
committed to destroying
No more toying around...like I did with
your no-good mama
Hmmm...maybe that's the past source
of our future drama
You WILL learn to obey the rules that
I set...believe that shit
And I don't feel the least bit bad for the
honor of teaching you the hard lessons
That's life, baby girl! It's what the hell
happens in the real world.
Come close and let me teach u...
just a little farther so I can reach you

"Hush lil baby...don't u cry"..."Or Grandma
Anita's gonna sock you in your other eye"
I can't control what happens to you
outside...but I determine the weather
in here
I rule with an iron hand...
using the tool I learned with...FEAR
The basement will hide our
hideous secrets

The washing machine will erase the
screams that stain your clothes
Because I hate at a level that u can't
describe...and no one would believe
I pass to you all the filth within me...now
u be the good toilet and receive

You are punished for deeds that you have
yet to do
And I blame you for all the sins that you
have yet to commit
I am so close to you...the roots of your life
began with me
So who is better positioned...
to find your beautiful face...and spit

CHAPTER SIX

Handcuffed to Freedom

The stabbing incident was the straw that broke the camel's back. I became extremely volatile inside, and people began to take notice. Slowly but surely, I was beginning to lose myself; I was no longer the quiet, sweet girl that everybody knew. I was book-smart, but I had become someone else on the inside—someone who felt that everyone was against me, especially my Grandma Anita. I was too young to understand that deep down she had her own turmoil and pain and that she was incapable of loving me or even realizing what she was doing to me. What I did know and understand was that if I stayed any longer, I may not have lived to see another year...so I ran.

I packed what little clothes, or rags, as Grandma Anita called them, and didn't look back. I took some of the loose change I had in my back pocket and took the bus across town to K-Mart, which would be my first stop because I was desperately in need of some clothes. K-Mart was centrally located in the McKinley High School district, across from a Denny's restaurant. Since I didn't have any money, I knew would have to return to boosting to get what I needed. I had never ventured into this particular type of store. When I was with the girls, we hit department stores, giving us multiple exit routes. K-Mart only had front-store exits doors. I probably could have talked myself out of the feat, but I was in too desperate of a situation, needing both clothes and food. Thus, I disregarded all the logistics, walked in the store, and went directly for the Juniors' section.

I followed through with my regular routine of going to the dressing room and putting on the clothes I was stealing underneath my own worn-out clothes. I walked out of the dressing room carrying only my book bag. I was in a hurry to leave the store and get something to eat. I was starving and only had a little money to get something to put in my belly. I made my way to the exit door.

"Excuse," me a voice behind me called out.

"Do you mind if I search your bag?" he asked.

"No," I said, thinking that perhaps he wouldn't.

"You know you've been caught on camera stealing, don't you?" he said, reaching for my book bag.

I swallowed hard. I could feel my heartbeat pulsating in my ears. The only thing that kept flashing in my mind was that the police would come and take me back to Grandma Anita. So in that instant, I decided not to give my name. I figured if they didn't know who I was then they couldn't take me back.

After searching my book bag, the plainclothes officer noticed a tag from the stolen merchandise, which was poorly concealed.

"The police have been called. We will have a female officer search you for stolen merchandise. So if you have anything on you, you need to give it up now."

"I do," I said, spilling the beans," I said, lifting up my shirt to reveal the stolen garment I had hidden. My hands were trembling uncontrollably. I had been caught and was in some serious trouble.

I was escorted to the bathroom and given the opportunity to give back the stolen items. The police arrived a short time later and took a statement from the store personnel. Then they approached me. By this time, I was sitting in a back area, outside from public view. A middle-aged-looking white male officer took charge.

"What's your name?" he said, in between his bubble gum chews.

"Tiffany."

"Tiffany, what?" he asked.

"Carter," I lied. It was the only thing I could think of at that particular time with my quick-witted nature. "But please don't take me back home," I said, now sobbing.

"Well, you're lucky," the officer said, between bubble gum chews once again.

The news warmed my heart, because even though I knew I had done wrong, I was elated in knowing that I would not be returning to 920 Lafayette. I was desperate to escape, and if it didn't work this time, I promised myself that I'd keep repeating my behavior until someone heard my cry.

"So where am I going?" I asked, fearing the answer.

"You'll be remanded to the Juvenile Detention Center on East Ferry. You'll have to appear before a judge."

I knew that if I didn't tell my real name, things would only get uglier. "My name is not Tiffany Carter," I blurted out.

"What's your real name?" the officer said, folding his arms as if he was beginning to lose his patience with me.

"Tiffany Duson....D.U.S.O.N," I said, sure that he'd ask how to spell my last name. Nearly everyone did.

"Why did you lie about your name?" the officer said.

My real reason was because I thought I could get away with doing so. But I knew I couldn't say that, so I just hunched my shoulders.

The female officer jotted down something on her tablet and then approached the two of us.

"Turn around and place your hands behind your back," she said, reaching for her cuffs.

My life had taken another turn...for the worse.

∞ ∞ ∞ ∞

Upon arrival at East Ferry, I was taken to a room and strip searched. When that was over, I was taken to a separate room where I was held for what they called processing. The floor was made of off-white concrete, and a plastic mattress lay in the middle of the floor. The room was cold. Determined not to even touch the mattress, I sat on the concrete floor in the far left corner of the room.

After processing was completed, I was moved to a cell and given a brief rundown on forthcoming protocol and procedures.

"You'll stay here until lunchtime. Then, you'll go before the judge," a young black corrections officer with the nametag "Bivins" said.

I was starving, so the mention of lunch was right down my alley; it's what I wanted to hear.

I nodded, and Officer Bivins closed the cell door and locked it. It hit me—I had truly lost my freedom. I suddenly had an urge to use the bathroom. I looked around the empty cell. There was an iron slate that stood out from the right side of the cell. I assumed it was the bed. There was a folded blanket on the top of the iron slate. It looked a bit more enticing than the dirty mattress in the other room, and I didn't want to stand, so I walked over to the slate, unfolded the blanket, and spread it over the slate. I sat at the edge for a few moments, testing the slate's strength. It didn't move or make any cracking sounds, so I thought it was pretty safe. I scooted back until my back was against the brick wall and closed my eyes.

The one thing about jail is that it provides you with time to think. That, I did. I thought about all of the things I had suffered through at such a young age. I even thought about my mother—Conitra. For all I knew, she could have been dead. But I began to wonder whether she had reinvented herself and her life. If so, what did they look like? What if she was an aspiring super model? After all, Granddad Carlos always told me that I was beautiful just like my mother. While I never saw myself as beautiful because I spent so much time feeling unloved and despised by Grandma Anita, I often pictured my mother as a beautiful woman. What I felt about her, however, was quite different from how I pictured her.

Later that afternoon, I appeared before a judge to answer to the charge of shoplifting. I pleaded innocent as directed by my court-appointed attorney, and a court date was set. I remember being dressed in a puke green pair of corduroy pants and a multi-colored turtleneck that had long sleeves to cover my scars. I caught a glimpse of Grandma Anita sitting in the back of the courtroom. I turned back to face the judge quickly.

I remember them classifying me as a juvenile delinquent, and, while I didn't know exactly what that meant, I knew that it wasn't a good thing. But nevertheless, after all the legal jargon and bargaining between the prosecutor and my public defender had ceased, I was permitted to go home with Grandma Anita. But after being given options by the Court to keep me, place me on court probation, or relinquish custody of me to the State of New York and be allowed monthly home visits on the weekends, she opted for the latter. I was relieved that my Grandma Anita took this route.

∞ ∞ ∞ ∞

After the red tape was cleared, which took about two days, I was released from East Ferry to an all-girls group home run by a lady dubbed "Sister McCall". Sister McCall arrived at the detention facility with two other girls to pick me up. She escorted me out of the facility to a dark green minivan. I got in the van, put on my seatbelt—a habit I got from Granddad Carlos—and made myself content. Any place was better than returning to 920 Lafayette.

We drove through familiar parts of town. When the car came to a permanent stop, my stomach began to churn. The group home was located around the corner from Buffalo General County Hospital, not too far from my original place of torment. From the minute I arrived, I knew the situation wasn't going to go well.

Sister McCall introduced me to her daughter, Candace, who, evident by the nasty frown on her face, wasn't too fond of her mother taking in another child.

Being in a new place also meant obeying a new set of rules. The school wasn't too far from our house, and we were all on a strict schedule. Every morning like clockwork, a loud voice yelled up the stairs at 6:00 am to wake us up. Breakfast was served promptly at 7:00 am. There were five females in the house, so getting ready in an hour with one bathroom was no small feat. Since all of us girls went to the same school, we all had to leave at the same time. Anyone who didn't make it out the door with the others would be forced to do extra chores later.

I went along with the routine for the first few days, but eventually I began to get homesick—as crazy as that sounds. I knew I was all mixed up because I didn't really want to go home, but I didn't want to be at the group home either. I didn't like being questioned about why I was there or any of my other personal life, for that matter.

"You just mind your own damn business," I told one of the girls.

"You ain't gotta be a bitch," she snapped back.

It took less than five seconds for me to jump all over her.

"Get off me," she screamed. "Get the f**k off me," she added, now pulling my hair.

Sister McCall came running upstairs and broke us up. "I told you girls that there's a zero tolerance for fighting," she said, her eyes moving back and forth between the two of us. "And since you're the last one to come, you'll be the first one to go. I just refuse to have a little nine-year old come up in here and disrupt my flow. I ain't no daggone referee to be breaking up constant arguments and fights."

I stood still just listening to the words leave her lips but not allowing them to truly penetrate my comprehension.

"Go on, get your things. I'm bringing you back to East Ferry," she said, walking away.

I was fine with leaving her place, but all I knew was that I wasn't going back to East Ferry. Sister McCall called the center to let them know that she was bringing me back, and then proceeded upstairs to pack my things, since I never even budged.

As soon as her feet hit the stairs, I hit the door. I took off into the night air with no jacket. I ran until I tripped on the sidewalk in front of Rite-Aid. I tried to run through the hospital parking lot but was stopped by a total stranger who was acting as if he were conducting a citizen's arrest.

"Get off of me," I screamed repeatedly. My screams got the attention of the hospital police who came over to see what all of the hoopla was about. Before he could sort out the situation, Candace pulled up and jumped out of the van. Apparently, Sis McCall had sent her out looking for me, and she had called the police, too.

"She's a runaway!" she told the police, walking up to me. "She was on her way back to the East Ferry's Detention Center, so she ran."

I hated Candace in that moment, not because she was squealing on me, but because she lacked total empathy or concern for me. We weren't too different, just had different circumstances in life. But I had been caught again, and I was finally starting to see that escaping was not going to be easy.

I went back to East Ferry. This time, I was locked up in the secure facility where all the Juvenile Delinquent III's were housed. It would be my home for the next week until I made my scheduled court appearance. This new facility was much more stringent than the one where I'd made my initial visit—there was absolutely no freedom. Every time we went outside, we were placed in handcuffs and chained to one another. In a short time, however, since my wrists were so small, I became infamous for sliding my hands out of the handcuffs. That's where I earned the nickname "String Bean." It only took a few of these episodes for the facilitators to become annoyed with my antics before they finally decided to place me not only in one full set of handcuffs, but also another set of shackles added to the arsenal.

The days went by slowly, and it was agonizing. But then, finally, my Wednesday court date arrived. When I arrived at court, I was placed in a room with other juvenile offenders until my case was called. Since Grandma Anita didn't have the money or the inclination to get me a lawyer, I was given another public defender.

When my case was called, I was escorted to the courtroom. I remember doing a quick glance of the courtroom and seeing the disgruntled look on Grandma Anita's face. She might as well not have shown up because she wasn't offering any type of emotional support. If anything, her presence made things worse— I feared her more than I feared the judge who held my fate.

I turned around quickly to face the judge as my charges were read—shoplifting, assault, resisting arrest, and a whole slew of other charges. Next, he read off a laundry list of incidences in my past history, presumably to serve as justification for what the "State of New York" was proposing as punishment.

"She's a burdensome, problematic, hostile, troubled child that has run away from home on several occasions. And this is from her own grandmother's statement," the prosecutor said, pointing at me as he read from the stapled papers he held.

It's ironic that Grandma Anita didn't disclose that she was the reason behind my runaway attempts. But despite having heard the mean, nasty words the prosecutor used to describe me, I tried not to show any emotion. I didn't want Grandma Anita to know that her words had just pierced my soul. I wouldn't be telling the truth, however, if I didn't feel betrayed by Grandma Anita, particularly when I thought of all the beatings, all the scars, and all the times that I went hungry—all the secrets I'd kept.

The rest of the process seemed like a blur to me. What really stood out was the final verdict. I was being committed the Tryon Residential Center for Girls, a state facility located upstate in Johnstown, New York. Rumor had it that Tryon was a facility in which little girls who were considered terrors and lacking in discipline were sent. By the time my attorney stood up to defend me, I had broken down in tears. It didn't matter, though; neither my tears nor his argument swayed the judge in the least bit. I was convicted, labeled as the prosecution had suggested, and given an immediate ship out date.

The damage was done, and there was no turning back. The homes were not fun, and I hadn't fled abuse and starvation to end up being pushed around, locked up, or told what to do. Unfortunately, like so many other aspects of my life, I had no choice. It was no longer a game, and my little "camping trip" was over. The handcuffs were placed back on me and the bailiff proceeded to lead me out of the courtroom. As if on cue from a movie director, Grandma Anita put on a performance, crying and yelling out to me.

"Tiff....Tiff....don't cry, baby."

She had never uttered such words of sentiment in all my days. My caramel-toned face turned red. I knew we crying for different reasons—she was acting; I was for real. But the guards stopped long enough for her to say good-bye to me.

"Stop all that crying," she said leaning in to wipe my tears away. "You went and did this to yourself. You'll be home soon enough."

I was icy inside. The only thing that was missing from that speech was to "keep my business to myself", but then she'd already violated that creed and it didn't really matter, not in that moment. Nevertheless, I was escorted out of the courtroom and back to the holding cell where the other juvenile offenders were being held. Since the bus only made one trip back to the center after all the court cases were over, I had a long wait ahead of me. While I sat there, I had plenty of time to think about my new status. I was officially a Ward of the State now—Grandma had given up all custodial rights to me.

∞ ∞ ∞ ∞

Nothing could have prepared me for the brutal invasion of privacy I experienced when I arrived at Tryon Juvenile Prison. As soon as I arrived, I was taken into a room, processed, and then stripped of any ties that I had to the "real world." My clothes were taken, and I was fitted for more of their fashionable apparel, only this time, it came in sets of six.

Looking like a true prisoner, I was taken into another room to meet with a group of counselors gave me the rundown on the new set of rules at Tryon—no talking unless spoken to; and when hungry, thirsty, or needing to go to the restroom, raise hand. I was allowed to use the phone once a week and mail call was nightly. This information didn't mean much to me, since I didn't really have anyone to call—Grandma Anita was hardly going to accept a collect call. As for the mail, I had no one to send me care packages, so that was also a non-issue.

Because of the tight security and the setup of the complex itself, I gave up on the idea of running away and came to terms with the fact that I would remain there for the next six months to a year. So I tried to settle into my new life. Classes were held daily on the campus, but we had to earn our freedom, as well as the privilege to be involved in other activities. Once you earned enough points and advanced to different levels, you were allowed to do more things. Unlike the other treatment facilities, I had grown to learn the system and necessary tricks of passing the time. I decided to get involved, put on all the right faces, and say the right things in order to gain my freedom sooner rather than later.

Within a few months, I had advanced to level three, which allowed me to walk around freely to a certain extent, except at nighttime. I could also partake in some of the offsite campus activities. It was here that I learned how to cross-country ski and partake in cross-country running, which became my new outlet. I'd run all the time. We'd run indoors and outdoors through the countryside.

Running also gave me a sense of just how far away from everything we actually were. I had no clue where I was; the land around me was barren, and I had to run for miles with the team just to see a barn or something that remotely resembled a house. Forget about seeing a store because there was none in sight.

Running became a great release and allowed me to count down my days. I was at Tryon for six months before my treatment plan was rewritten, and it, in and of itself, was a feat of my own doing. I'd had no contact with my family and had managed to suppress my resentment for them enough to fool the doctors. All sessions went something like this:

"Were you ever abused?" they would ask, flashing cards in my face to see where my head was.

"No," I'd answer, matter-of-factly.

"Were you ever raped?"

"No," I'd lie.

Today, when I look back on those sessions, I wish I would have those questions truthfully. I would have probably received the proper intervention needed to cope. Because I didn't, however, I became an angry child who wanted the world to feel my pain. I got slick and sneaky and knew how to conceal it all. My cunning allowed me to be approved for early release, and I completed the remainder my time in a less secure facility. I was elated.

I was approaching eleven years of age, and I thought that meant I'd soon be returning back to Buffalo. Instead, I was told that I would be going to Gateway, a Methodist Home for Children) in Williamsville, NY where I would get further counseling and be evaluated for long-term foster care. I didn't have the wherewithal to put all of the pieces together, but I felt that it had to be better than remaining at Tryon. I was tired of asking permission to relieve myself and feed my face, so I was game for whatever leaving that place meant. I was also told that visits with my grandmother would be reestablished, the long-term plan being, to integrate me back into my family environment. Hell, whatever that meant. But I was optimistic. As far as I was concerned, there was still hope, and I had faith that my getting older meant less abuse, perhaps no more beatings. Perhaps Grandma Anita had even turned into a rational human being.

Whatever it meant, I could finally see a light at the end of a very dark road, and I was praying that it wasn't the dead end that it had started out to be. I knew I couldn't go another ten years down the same path. It was time to make a change. It was during this time, when I had all the privileges of my life taken away from me, that I realized just how much I took even the simple pleasure and privilege to use the bathroom for granted. You'll never understand what it's like to be locked down and in a dark place until you've lost your freedom—lost your ability to interact with the outside world. When no one calls to see if your sanity is still in check, when no letters or

Hallmark cards come, and the moments of feeling like you have a purpose have been depleted from your spirit, it is when you truly come to grips with the loss of your freedom.

∞ ∞ ∞ ∞

When I arrived at Gateway, I felt as if it were time to start running again. I did not want to go to another foster home, did not want to return home, nor did I really want to be at Gateway. The atmosphere at Gateway was about as normal as it could be. After all, it was an institution, so there was only so much that I could do. I ate, slept, played spades, and watched TV with the other boys and girls. We were allowed to decorate our rooms as we pleased, for the most part. So the walls in most of our rooms were plastered with posters, magazine pictures, and hand-drawn artifacts of hip-hop artists and bands and Bernard Gill.

Lots of things about me were changing, especially my physical appearance. I was starting to look like a young adult, probably a sixteen-year old, instead of a twelve year old.

So my chances of being taking in by a loving family just dying to adopt a little

154

black girl, were slim to none. But despite not being in the "ideal" situation, I learned that some family was interested in taking me in. The counselor wanted to place me in a group home monitored by them for a month to see how well I transitioned before making a more permanent arrangement for me. This meant returning to the infamous "Sister McCall's home." I figured that the experience would be pretty interesting, particularly since I was almost two years older and my attitude had changed slightly. I agreed to the trial period and returned to her home.

Sister McCall knew the family that was interested in taking me in. She was given the liberty of introducing us to one another. On our way over to the Mason's house, she gave me the rundown on the family. There was Mr. and Mrs. Mason ad three children—two boys and one girl.

"You'll be going to church quite a bit with the Masons because they are churchgoing folk," she said, with a sly grin.

I couldn't ever recall stepping into a church, so I didn't have any predispositions about going, either way—good or bad. I also thought it was pretty funny that Sister McCall was telling me all these things, as if I had some kind of say in the matter. I didn't, of course. I was the one who simply had to be there, be moved, and do as I was told. There truly was no other option.

I listened to Sister McCall ramble, not really paying close attention to what she was saying. The minivan
came to a stop once we pulled up in front of the house.
I looked up. The house was a horrible-looking cran-
berry and yellow thing. It had a front porch and a long
driveway that led up to a shed in the backyard. We were
told that we had to enter the house through the side
door. When we went in through the side door, there was
a set of stairs that downstairs to a basement. To the right
was a separate set of stairs that led to the kitchen, living room, formal dining room, and bedrooms. The house
was huge on the inside, although the outside was an aes-
thetic nightmare.

I was introduced to the Mason family and given
a quick tour of the house. I was shown what would soon
be my new room. The walls were painted green with
flowers around the border, and white lace curtains hung
from the window. Not quite appealing, but a vast difference from the cell I lived in at Tryon.

When I first met the Masons, I remember thinking
that there seemed to be something earthy about them.
Mrs. Mason appeared to be proper and prim, and she
spoke eloquently, enunciating all her T's and I's and E's.
Mrs. Mason took me on a tour of the rest of the house.

I met Kevin and Edmond Jr, the two sons. Kevin was
a senior in high school, and Edmond Jr. was in his junior year of high school. Karisma, the daughter, was in
the second grade. Everyone seemed receptive, but when

I met Karisma I knew that she and I would probably not get along so well. Then, I met the last member of the family—Mr. Mason. He was COGIC minister and had a way about him that let you know he was no-nonsense.

I was invited to join the family for dinner that evening. I didn't know whether to be excited or scared. I also wasn't sure that I really wanted to stay, so I told them that I wasn't hungry.

The next day, a social worker visited me from Gateway. She inquired how my initial visit with the Mason's went. I had grown tired of Gateway, weary of being shifted from home to home and scared stiff of returning to another treatment center. Here was a family that actually wanted me, and while I remained leery of their intentions, I made up in my mind that I wanted something different. I wanted a family. While I grew up in instability, I knew I needed stability that more than anything. At some point, the deal was sealed, and a week later I was spending my first night with the Masons.

I was able to get a better picture of all of the Masons during my first few days in their home. Mrs. Mason was the psychologist of the family. She analyzed everything and was always looking for ways to resolve matters with the usage of words. She believed in teaching her children how to resolve issues without conflict. She stood about 5'7", wore glasses, and had jet black hair. She was an evangelist and was also an avid lover of the arts.

The degenerative disorder Parkinson's disease ran in the Mason family, and at that time, Mrs. Mason's mother was very ill and confined to a bed. She could not feed herself, use the facilities on her own, or talk clearly Even though she could speak, it appeared to be a language that only Mrs. Mason could understand and thus interpret for others. My view of Mr. Mason didn't change much. He was a tough father figure. He laid down the law from the very beginning.

"There'll be no lying, stealing, or talking back up in this house. Church services are attended by all three times a week, no exceptions but death. We believe in fair labor. Meaning, we take turns with chores around here. There's no television and you must study scripture twice a week. These are the house rules. Now, you can take'em or leave'em," he said, matter-of-factly.

As I listened to him drone on, I got a flashback of my time at the girls' home. *Can I really handle someone telling me what I can and cannot do?* I wondered.

I tried to blend in as best as I could. I was registered in a public school and had no problems adapting to the environment. I gravitated toward the honor roll quite quickly, wanting to impress the Masons. Emotionally, they had done more for me in months than my grandmother hadn't accomplished my entire life. Cognizant of this fact, I became reluctant to return to 920 Lafayette, even for a visit.

Despite the best of everyone's intentions, living with the Mason's had its bumps and bruises. I took a lot of pride in my hair, and I was bothered that Mrs. Mason was incapable of doing my hair the way my Grandma Anita used to do it. It wasn't always neat, some ponytails weren't the same size, and it made me furious. Upset one day over Mrs. Mason's refusal to do my hair over, I locked myself in the bathroom, opened the medicine cabinet, took the scissors out, and chopped my hair off. Remnants of the hair that used to hang down the middle of my back lay on the bathroom floor. I was bald and ponytail-less. To make matters worse, Mrs. Mason vowed to take me to the hairdresser from then on. My plan on getting attention and an animated response had backfired.

That afternoon in 1988 proved to be one of the worst days of my life. Mrs. Mason forced me to get a Jheri Curl. I was disgusted and thought that that had to be the worst form of punishment I could ever have received. I could not take the smell of the chemicals, the oil dripping down my forehead, or the activator on my pillows. I wasn't only angry, I was more so embarrassed. I wanted no parts of that hair revolution. Momma told me that it looked beautiful and that I would no longer have to worry about my hair again. But that was easy for her to say. As you could imagine, the kids in school were as cruel as an episode of Saturday Night Live. I became the talk of the school and the source of great material for the biggest tease-fest on the upper east side of New York. I earned the new nickname, Tweety Bird.

I came home from school after the first day with my new "do," went to the bathroom and threw a fit along with my violin, which went flying out the window shortly thereafter. I went on what I considered to be my last visit with my grandmother, who literally cried when she saw my hair. But when I told her what had truly happened, she switched gears and began to laugh hysterically. She was laughing all while pretending to care. This Dr. Jekyll and Mr. Hyde behavior had become routine with her.

"That's what you get for inviting them white folks up in our business. Stayed your fast tail at home, you wouldn't be going through none of this mess," she said, throwing a rag at me to catch.

I caught the rag and folded it over. I never said too much of anything, but on the inside, I was hurting bad.

By this time, Grandma Anita was the only one living in the house. Aunt Denise and Garry had moved away again and were now living on the west side of the city in their own apartment. So with everyone gone, Grandma Anita pretty much had the house to herself with an occasional visitor from time to time. Granddad Carlos had been gone, for over four years, and it was obvious that Grandma Anita was on her way out as well. Grandma Anita's arthritis was really bad, and she complained that it was preparing to rain because she was feeling it in her bones and not feeling much like herself.

This visit was reminiscent of the old times with Grandma Anita. As always, I ran her errands, played her lotto numbers, picked up groceries, cashed in some food stamps to get her some money, and even ironed the curtains that she had starched a few days prior.

It was apparent that not much had changed. Grandma Anita still had her soap opera routine, resting in her old chair. I sat on the floor in the same spot I had been conditioned to sit in a few years earlier, mainly out of habit. My butt print was still ingrained there and served as a reminder of everything I'd suffered within those walls. I stayed with her for the day, returning home the next day to the Mason's as scheduled. I knew when I left that I didn't want to return and that there was nothing that could have brought me back.

Spell families without the "lies"

Just try...
See if you can separate the fact
that all families...end with lies
Whether it's the deceptions that
are being openly told
Or that wealth of deposits that
lies beneath

Because I have seen the consequences
of burying the truth
I have believed things that have no basis
in reality
Yet they are a valid part of my mentality
Sometimes words are used to get the
things that u want
...even if it's not what u should have
Tools to twist the truth until it conforms
to a shape it's not intended to make
Like leaves and dog feces gathered
together in a pile...by the same rake
Venom dripping from the most spiteful
tongues...hidden behind fake smiles

Lies...that coat the intestines of a home...
and corrupt and infest it with bile

But what of the rich deposit that lies
hidden beneath the surface
And must be mined with hard labor
to yield its lucrative fruit
Like the mother or father that lies on
their face...praying over their children
These are lies that honor God and
family...the heart of happiness' pursuit
A rich oil deposit...it can be easily walked
over...because it runs so deep
Covered by hardness...hard life...hard
choices...hard battles
But find it, and it will affect the wealth
of the whole territory
It will change the lives of all those around
It pays back many times over...Every
promise is reaped as a vow

Oh yes...we all lie for our family
...the only question is how.

She Speaks

CHAPTER SEVEN

Defying the Odds

From 1988-1991, I was on a mission to defy the odds stacked up against me. I burned my wheels trying to ignore what everyone said about me, refusing to believe what anyone said I would become, according to statistics. I stayed in therapy, but I thought the doctors who were treating me were as crazy as I pretended to be. Though they constantly tried to tap into my emotions, I simply didn't allow them to do so. I was only there because the State said I had to have counseling. I listened but made no honest attempt to apply anything to my life. I couldn't make a connection with the therapists, and I didn't believe that they were really interested in me or that they truly cared.

They asked the same mundane questions session after session—How are you? My mouth uttered calculated responses, but my inner voice screamed "Save me!" I learned early on in the sessions that I was judged what I felt and how I responded. So since these were the same individuals who had the power to decide my fate, I became a master at keeping things close to the belt and giving them just enough information that would give the illusion of progress.

In the weeks and months that followed, I learned a lot about myself. My escapades would end up almost costing me the only stability I'd ever known. Though I was supposed to be on a pattern of reformation, by the time I was thirteen I had reverted back to some of my bad habits and was trying to incorporate them into my lifestyle inside of the Mason home.

I had been living with the Mason's for about a year and a half and had pretty much fallen into their routine. Mr. Mason's day consisted of working at the church, fixing up his car, and volunteering his time to work with seniors. He'd leave early in the morning and would return in the evening after 5:00 pm. Mrs. Mason was an educator and worked with adults who had not completed high school and wanted to obtain profitable careers. She had a way with getting people to maximize their potential, the same gift she used to teach me how to embrace adversity and become more accepting of myself.

Mr. Mason liked to collect coins, mostly silver dollars and fifty-cent pieces. In fact, he had cans of them tucked away in his bedroom closet. Many of them dated back as far as 1875, which made their worth valuable. It was never said to any of us that we weren't allowed to touch his collection; some things just didn't need to be verbalized—or did they? I can't truly say it would have made a difference if anyone had verbalized the restriction or not. My actions revolved around my constant need for acceptance by my peers and being envied by my family. I wanted them to see me doing much better than them, without having them in my life.

I had scouted the local pawnshop and made some inquires about the coins' value. My initial thoughts were to only take a couple of Mr. Mason's coins, just so I could have a little money in my pocket. I was teased in school a lot because of the way that I dressed. The other kids said that I looked frumpy and plain and that my clothes looked as though they came from the Goodwill. So I wanted to project an image that would be acceptable to my peers, starting by changing the way I dressed. I liked the Mason family, in general, but I felt as though their traditional lifestyle was hindering me from fitting in. So, one day while Mr. Mason was in the shower, I snuck into his closet and took as many coins as I could get my hands on. I skipped school that day and headed over to the pawnshop. I pawned six coins and got well over two hundred dollars for them. With money in hand, I took the train to the mall and went shopping. I topped it off by treating myself to lunch at McDonald's, and then hopped back on the train in an effort to get home around the same time that school let out.

When I got home, I played cool as if nothing had happened. I went through the motions of my afternoon routine, practicing the violin while Karisma practiced the piano. Even at the dinner table, things seemed normal, normal for the Mason family, that is. We ate dinner and ended the night with our baths, prayer, and our usual reading of scriptures from the Bible. By 8:00 pm, the children were sent to our rooms to get ready for bed.

I was awakened out of my sleep by Mrs. Mason, which took me for a loop. "Papa wants to see you downstairs," she said.

I knew in that instant that I had been caught. I hadn't rehearsed an excuse, or a lie, which is what any excuse I tried to muster up would have been. Naturally, I was a bit grumpy, but I slid out of the bed and headed downstairs. Mrs. Mason following after me.

The empty can was sitting square in the middle of the table when I pushed the half-cracked door open. My stomach churned, and I felt sick.

"Have a seat," Mr. Mason instructed as if he was getting ready to deliver a sermon of some sorts.

Hesitantly, I complied. Mrs. Mason sat down next to Mr. Mason.

"Do you know how long I was saving those coins?"

I hunched my shoulders. It wasn't that I didn't care, I just didn't know the answer to his question.

"You know, forget it. I'm not going to get into that. But I want you to know that what you've done has really hurt me. It's like you've taken a knife and stabbed us in the back."

I raised my eyebrows. I hadn't stolen from anyone else but Mr. Mason.

"Yes, when you steal out of someone's home, you're robbing the whole family, essentially."

"I'm sorry," I said in a tone just above a whisper.

"I'm just curious, are you truly sorry or are you sorry you got caught?"

"Truly sorry," I mumbled.

"I mean, after all we've done—taking you into our home when no one else wanted to—"

That was all it took for me to start crying. He was using that infamous line that gave me the rag doll feeling that Grandma Anita had instilled in me, a vivid reminder that my mother had thrown me away. I was way too young to formulate expressions for what I was truly feeling and dealing with. On one hand, yes, I wanted nice things, but more than that, I wanted to belong, to fit in somewhere. I wanted to disprove someone else's prophecy of failure. I just didn't know how to go about achieving them. So while my true intent was genuine, the route I took to accomplish it, was self-destructive.

"Tears aren't going to work now, Tiffany. You've betrayed us, stolen from us. In all my life, I've never had one of my kids take anything from me—" he paused and shook his head as if he still couldn't believe what I had done. Mrs. Mason, who I called Mama by this time, didn't say a word; she simply nodded and concurred with everything Mr. Mason said. "Well, I'm not about have a thief in my home now. I'll be calling Gateway tomorrow. You're going to have to leave," he followed up with.

"Go back up to your room. Your things will be packed in the morning so you can leave," Mrs. Mason said, rubbing Mr. Mason's right hand.

I could tell that the decision to send me back was not an easy one. But they had lost trust in me, which was apparently, a deal breaker. So mournfully, I went back upstairs. I just knew it was over for me. Mr. Mason was tough and appeared to be unforgiving. I climbed into my bed and cried myself to back to sleep that night.

By breakfast time, Karisma, Kevin, and Edmond, Jr. knew about what I had done. Mr. Mason had long gone to work, which made sitting at the table more tolerable for me. I don't think I could have looked at him so sooner after being confronted. I was contrite and indeed ashamed of what I had done. Mrs. Mason didn't say much, she carried her influence in a discretionary manner; it was never on display for the viewing public. That's the one thing I loved about Mrs. Mason, her compassion was undeniable.

"I'm going to try and talk to Papa when he comes home, but I'm pretty sure his mind is made up. You really broke his heart."

I didn't need her to tell me that I'd let him down in a big way; I knew it. But I went on to school that day, unable to focus. The only thing I could think about was returning back to the hell that I had come out of two years earlier.

There's no doubt in my mind that God played a role in the Masons rendering forgiveness unto me. I had really messed up bad. But with them willing to give me a second chance, I vowed not to disappoint them again. After all, I considered them Momma and Papa; they were, by far, the best examples of parents in my life. Although Granddad Carlos played a significant role in my early years, his efforts were often thwarted by the mean attacks of Grandma Anita.

My parents agreed with the notion that I needed to heal, and start anew. If there was one thing I had learned from Grandma Anita, it was how to shift my emotions seamlessly at times. Letting go meant leaving the Duson-Gibson-Robinson family in the past.

∞ ∞ ∞ ∞

I was on top of the world my last year of junior high school. I was even beginning to make good friends. Quite naturally for me, it was with a group of other misfits and outcasts. Mama Mason had been back and forth to the school board trying to stop them from holding me back and labeling me as "slow." The school administration tried to use my experiences in girls' homes and the fact that I was emotional at times as an excuse to hold me back, saying that I could not learn in a regular class environment. But Mama Mason was not having it. If there was one thing she could do, it was challenge systems. She used her education and smarts to successfully make the argument that my only problem with the class work was that it was not challenging enough for me and that my boredom was not a sign of retardation or "slowness." I was the same child who had skipped the fourth grade and made the honor roll on a consistent basis.

When everything was said and done, Mamma had beaten the entire school system at its own game and even had me enrolled in the honor society in that same year. This gave me some confidence. I was moving beyond the stereotypes that had been placed on me. I got closer to Papa, and Karisma and I bonded on another level. In fact, she had officially branded me as her big sister. The Masons tried to adopt me again, but Grandma Anita objected. Because of our blood ties, she was still consulted on matters pertaining to me. I didn't need papers, though, to know who my real parents were. Olivia was my Mama and Edmond, Sr. was my Papa. Papers or not, I was a member of the Mason family. Point blank.

By the time I was fourteen, I had entered into my sophomore year of high school and had developed my first real crush on the neighborhood pizza boy, Mark. He had a butter caramel complexion, stood about six feet tall, and drove a Mazda 626. Papa ordered pizza once a week from a local mom and pop shop, and Mark was

always the one who took our orders and delivered pizza to our house. One day I decided to walk to the pizza shop after school and hang out with him.

Mark and I clicked immediately. He became the first boy ever to kiss me. Deep down, I had attachment issues, and it was clear that I was searching for another kind of connection when I met Mark. I had always wanted to find my biological father and understand why things were the way they were, and I had the same yearning in my spirit for my biological mother.

Although I had two people who took on the role of great parents and loved me dearly, I craved normalcy. So I made up stories to keep from having to tell the truth as to why I was in foster care. I confided in Mark and told him snippets about my past. I was excited about my friendship with Mark, and I wanted to share my feelings with someone, so I decided to confide in Papa. So one afternoon, while we were sitting outside on the front porch I mustered up the courage to talk to him.

"Hey, Papa, guess what!"

"Yep," he replied, looking up from the newspaper he was reading.

"I met a boy," I said shyly.

He frowned. "What boy? Not in this house."

"But it's Mark, the pizza guy."

"I said, no dating, at least not until you're at least sixteen. Besides, he's too old for you. Keep your head in the books and outta the streets."

And that was it. The conversation was cut short. He didn't like Mark and had no reservations about making his opinion of him known.

I pretended to concede and told my Papa that I would not see Mark anymore. That seemed easy. The hard part, however, was letting Mark in on the decision. Knowing that it was something I had to do in person, I arranged to meet Mark one last time.

I told Papa I was going to the library to study after school. Instead, I walked to the pizza shop where Mark worked. He was in the back area, so I waited up front.

"Hey, gorgeous," he said, when he recognized me.

I smiled. Mark called me all sorts of sweet names—gorgeous, precious, diamond, and the list went on.

"I'm gonna take my break. Hold on a sec while I clock out," he said, taking off his apron.

My heart raced—for two different reasons. I was growing madly in love with Mark, and on the other hand, I knew our time together had to come to an end, if I wanted to stay in the Mason home.

"So how was school?" he said, reaching for my hand. Mark was affectionate, and affection was something brand new to me. It felt good, and I didn't want to let it go. The wrestle within was real.

I wiped the sweat from my forehead.

"You hot?" he asked, perturbed by the outbreak of sweat pebbles forming on my forehead and cheeks.

"Kinda," I said, wiping my forehead once again. There was truly no easy way to say it, so I just came out with it. "Papa said I can't see you anymore."

"Why?" he said, looking into my eyes.

"He said you're too old and I'm too young."

"Ah, just one talk with the good ole Rev. and he'll change his mind," Mark said, making light of the matter. "Don't worry. It's gonna be all right. I'll prove to your pops that I'm a good guy," he said, squeezing my cheeks with his hands.

∞ ∞ ∞ ∞

A few days later, Mark pulled up to our home unannounced. As promised, he came to speak with Papa. He wanted to prove to Papa that he wasn't a bad boy and did indeed care about me.

I stood inside the door but watched nervously as Mark approached the front porch where Papa was sitting.

"Good afternoon, Reverend Mason," Mark said, reaching his right hand out to shake Papa's and hold a pizza box in his left hand.

"Good afternoon," Papa said, peering over his reading glasses and reluctantly extending his hand.

"Go on and get the pizza from him, Tiffany," Mama said, opening the front door. I stepped onto the porch and reached my hands out for the pizza. Taking his attention from Papa, Mark looked over at me and winked. I smiled sheepishly, feeling similar to Whoopi Goldberg in the Color Purple. Mark handed me the pizza and I turned to go back into the house, closing only the screen door but leaving the main door open so I could eavesdrop.

From the kitchen, I could hear the two of them engage in animated dialogue at times. Things would quiet down, and then heat back up again. I even overheard Papa quoting a few scriptures. Although I was never privy to all of specifics of their conversation, in my book, Mark had some brownie points just for having the gall to come speak with Papa. It drew me to him even more.

At the end of Mark and Papa's one-on-one, Papa still held on to his initial mandate—no dating. I was attracted to Mark's "bad boy" persona, and I liked the fact that he was older and did indeed have a car. In my book, Mark could have chosen someone else, particularly an older girl who didn't have to go through her daddy to date. I was so convinced that I meant something special to him, because he was going through leaps and bounds just to be able to date me. I didn't want to give up the euphoric high that I had developed in that short period of time, and neither did I want to give up Mark. So I made up in my mind that I would give up either.

Sometime during the third week of high school, Mark and I planned to meet up. He drove to the school to pick me up. I said good-bye to my crew and hopped in his car. We went back to his place, a small, cozy one-bedroom apartment located not too far from my high school. We ate pizza and chips and soon made our way over to the sofa where we cuddled up together to watch television. *This is a grown up relationship,* I thought. I was used to seeing my aunts and their boyfriends cuddled up on the sofa at 920 Lafayette.

It wouldn't be long before Mark's hands were all over my body. I pretended that I had to use the bathroom, just so I could interrupt the flow of things. But the moment I came sat back down on the sofa, Mark picked up where he left off.

"Stop it. I don't know if I want to go there with you... not now."

Mark stopped in the middle of trying to put his hands down my pants. "What did you think you were coming over here for?"

"To eat and hang out?" I said, asking more so than making a statement.

He chuckled. "Get with the times, Tiffany. Everybody's doing it, even the good ole church girls like yourself."

"I just don't know if I'm ready yet."

"Tiffany, you're not no damn virgin. What are you afraid of?"

"Nothing," I said. I wasn't a virgin, but I hadn't engaged in consensual sex before.

"Well, I'll tell you what, if you think I'm gonna stay around and you ain't giving up nothing, you can forget it. There's plenty of girls willing and able, giving me no reason to sit around and wait for you!" He was mad and agitated by this time.

Papa was right. Mark was too old for me. He thought a lot like the dirty old men I used to run from when I was a little girl. Before I could say anything else, he jumped up and walked out the front room. The phone rang and Mark answered. I stood up and fixed my clothes. I could hear him talking from the back bedroom but couldn't decipher exactly what he was saying. Moments later, however, he walked back in the room and grabbed his keys off the edge of the sofa where he had placed them.

"You gotta go. I have an emergency with my girls."

I didn't ask any prying questions, and I'm not sure I truly believed what he had just said. Nevertheless, the call was a welcomed interruption, so I reached down for my book bag and walked over to the door. Mark didn't follow behind me though.

"You not gonna bring me home?"

"Can't. Ain't got the time," he said, swinging the key ring around his index right index finger.

"Mark, how am I supposed to get home?" I asked in a moment of growing anxiety.

"Don't your oldest brother drive? Call him," he said, nonchalantly.

"I can't call anyone from home because I'm not supposed to be with you, remember?"

"Well, not my problem. This ain't gonna work anyway. So we can just call it quits right here."

I couldn't believe my ears. I was disposable within a matter of seconds, just because I didn't want to give up my body. In that very instant, I felt that familiar feeling of rejection. I'd dealt with abandonment all my life, and there it was happening to me again. I couldn't take it. I broke down in tears and begged Mark not to leave me. He looked at me and laughed.

"I don't deal with crazy bitches. You need to find a way home, too, because I ain't taking your ass."

"Can I at least use your phone to call my Mama," I said, tearfully.

"Go ahead," he said, reaching over and throwing the phone at me.

I was definitely seeing a different Mark—the Mark Papa tried to warn me about. With no one else to call, I broke down and called my mother, who in turn told my father and brothers. Kevin ended up coming to get me. The whole ride home was torturous.

"See, niggas ain't shit. They only want one thing. They get it, and then they're gone." Kevin taunted.

I nodded. I was both humiliated and hurt.

"Don't worry, sis. I'm gonna find somebody to whoop his ass for you. He won't even know where it's coming from. He still work at that pizza joint?"

I nodded once again. For some reason, I couldn't talk audibly, my tears did all the talking for me.

Points of Interest

Your fight is not my fight...but you'd
better fight well
Your story is your own...but who better
to tell?
Your pain can't be compared to
another's...cuz all bring hurt
Don't laugh at my soiled rags...just
because yours are free from dirt
Check that beam in your own eye...before
getting out the toothpick in mine
Are you willing to help me look?...then
don't be surprised that I don't find

My journey is made for my feet...your
steps have to walk their own path
Add up all your experiences...then
subtract all the "things" that you have
You'll be left with who you really are...not
that person you show to others
Free yourself from unnatural weights...
and from anything that smothers

Do what's in you to do
Find the route that you are meant to take
Don't worry about getting every
step right

Follow hard...and you'll override any
mistakes

Be like the camera...
Find your subject...get the right thing in
your view
Now adjust the focus...or else how can
you see clearly, what next to do?
Then take the picture...hold fast to the
decision you made
And choose what to save to your memory
card...and let everything else fade

Your fight is not my fight...and you really
don't have to fight well
But however you decide...know that your
circumstances will always willingly tell

CHAPTER EIGHT

Departing the Dessert

Moving forward to the spring of 1992, a few months shy of my 16th birthday, the State decided that it was time for them to cut me loose and grant me emancipation. So on June 1, 1992, I turned sixteen and was legally emancipated. My records were sealed, and I was given a new lease on life. Mom and Papa volunteered to help me transition into the 'real world'. They owned houses on the east side of the city. The neighborhoods weren't so great, but I'd have my own apartment, and I was elated. Momma and I agreed that I would pay two hundred dollars a month for rent and utilities, and it wasn't long before 45 Montana Avenue became my new place of independence.

Newly emancipated, I went to the welfare office and signed up for cash aid, Medicare, and food stamps. I was proud of myself. Though Papa wouldn't out-right admit it, I could tell he was sad to see me go. I was happy to have my parents support, but I was also happy to leave and venture out on my own.

By this time, Edmond, Jr. had gone to college and joined the Army Reserves. Kevin became a daddy to a baby boy, by his longtime girlfriend, Tracy, and had also moved out of the house. I had waited years for my turn, and with one year of high school left, I was feeling pretty good. My baby sister, Karisma, however, still had four more years to go.

Though I'd moved out of 46 Monticello place, I remained enrolled at Kensington High School, and in the fall of 1992, I returned to finish what I had start-ed. I was a junior, and it was important to me to finish my school, especially since my mother hadn't. I was determined to have a different life than the Duson wom-en. So I stayed on top of my studies and never missed a day, even when I had to schlep through the snow and rain. School was my only priority, and I had to get there.

Momma would pick me up for church each weekend, so I maintained my ties in church.

I obtained my work permit and landed a job at Ponderosa restaurant on a part-time basis to cover some of my bills and sustain myself. I established an entire new group of friends once people found out that I lived on my own. My place became a local hangout spot. Between the food I brought home from Ponderosa and what I bought with my food stamps, I made sure that there was always food in my cupboard. Looking back, I realize that these newfound friends didn't care as much about me as they did my kitchen, cable, Corn Pops, and corn on the cob. I so preoccupied with finishing school, aspiring to graduate with honors.

While working at Ponderosa, I met a man named Charles. He was a handsome black man who hailed from the Island of Haiti. He was eight years older than I, but it didn't matter all that much to me. He was an absolute gentleman in every sense of the word. He was studying psychology in his graduate degree program at the University of Buffalo. Charles worked at Ponderosa as a means of paying to his way through school.

Papa had given me the 4-1-1 on men, and his advice combined with what I had observed via Granddad Carlos, the men who were in and out of my aunties' lives, and the critter, Mark, I thought I had a good enough handle on how to take care of myself in the dating arena.

Charles was an absolute romantic. He'd drive me home after work and always remained a complete gentleman, never overstepping his boundaries. He wined and dined me and took me to the finest restaurants, bought me greeting cards and roses on every whim, and even sent me a sing-o-gram one Valentine's Day. He was good at surprises and kept a smile on my face by doing the simplest of things.

Charles had his own apartment off campus where he and several other Haitian Nationals lived. On the weekends, he would prepare dinner for me and take me on outings to the park, museums, and to the movies when I wasn't studying or doing other things with my family. During school breaks, he would travel back and forth to Florida to visit his elderly mother. Before I knew it, Charles and I fell in love, and we made no bones about it. We had been dating for almost a year, and he had not touched me, with the exception of random kisses on the cheek from time to time. During spring break of 1993, Charles introduced me to his family. His mother adored me, and his sister Nettie and I became good friends as well as shopping buddies. I just knew that Charles and I were meant to be, and I fought hard to keep things this way.

I opted not to take Charles home to meet my family. I had other plans, like going to college, and I was nervous as to how it was all going to play out. I loved hard and had possessive tendencies, which did more harm than any good. Even with my foster family as a surrogate, I still found myself craving affection and longing for a healthy family environment. The lack thereof left me emotionally depleted causing me to rely on the men and even women who came into my life to fill these voids. Charles was no exception. The thought of losing him scared me, so I held onto him like crazy glue, trying to control his every move. It was that possessive part of me that scared him and created an unhealthy dynamic for us both. Before long, he starting detaching himself from the relationship. Although I wanted to ignore this reality and remain in denial, I was forced to deal with our truth.

The message left on my answering machine one day brought things to an immediate head.

"Tiffany, you don't know me. My name is Michele... and I'm Charles's girlfriend."

I hit the Stop button. My heart was pounding fast. A flush of heat penetrated my cheeks. *Had I been played once again?*

Out of curiosity, I called the number back. The same voice on the machine answered the call.

"Michele?" I said, trying to confirm.

"This is Michele," the voice on the other end answered.

"It's Tiffany. You left me a message?"

"Yeah, I did. Have you been seeing Charles?"

"We've been dating for about a seven months now," I said counting back the time in my head.

"I take it he didn't tell you that he had a girlfriend."

"No, he didn't," I said, flopping down on the edge of my bed. My knees felt weak and could no longer support the weight on my body.

"Well, if you know Charles like I do, he's never going to own up to his actions. They only way he will is if we both confront him."

With adding instigation, Michele managed to convince me to agree to meet her at Charles's apartment. My initial instincts cautioned me against doing so—it was just plain ole dangerous in this day in time. Illogically, however, my need to confront Charles took precedence, and I agreed to meet this woman at Charles's apartment.

I would learn more about myself than I would about Charles by having agreed to confront him. Although I feared rejection, deep down I wanted to know if he would choose me over this Michele woman. But I was torn. On one end, if I stayed with the two-timer, it symbolized my weakness. If I walked away, it symbolized my strength. Neither of the two scenarios were enticing, however, because at the end of the day, my inner demons were still going to torment me. If I wasn't careful, I'd replace Charles with another undeserving man just as I had replaced Mark with Charles. It was the same vicious cycle the Duson women had gone through.

∞ ∞ ∞ ∞

Trying to get over the break up with Charles is when I started "cutting". Cutting is the term they use when people intentionally cut themselves. Psychologists say it's a coping mechanism of some sort. I've never fully understood the theory, but undoubtedly, it must hold some validity, because those who are psychologically damaged end up at some point in their lives, cutting.

One night, I grabbed a steak knife from the kitchen drawer and sat in the middle of the kitchen floor. I jabbed the knife into the skin on my inner left arm as hard as I could without necessarily severing a vein. I watched as the blood oozed out and down my arm onto the floor. I remember feeling a burning sensation, but it was in no way a comparison to the emotional pain I was feeling. So I switched the knife to my left hand and jabbed it into my inner right arm, just below the elbow. Again, I watched the blood ooze out onto my arm and onto the floor.

As I sat on my kitchen floor, I reminisced back over my life. I had endured a lot in my nearly seventeen years of life—abandonment, abuse, rape, incarceration, multiple episodes of deceit and rejection, etc. The list went on. But more importantly, I realized that I somehow managed to get back up, both literally and figuratively, and keep living. Somewhere deep down I realized that I was going nowhere slowly. The one thing

I did have that could change my fate was book smarts. Academics were the key to my success. And that night, I decided that I was going to pursue my academics in my pursuit for a better life.

I don't pretend to understand the true dynamics of the power of the mind, but I can attest to the fact that a made up mind is very powerful. I shifted gears, putting Mark, Charles, and Grandma Anita and the related trauma and drama behind. I decided to attend college. My grades were outstanding, so I applied to outstanding colleges such as Canisius, Virginia Union, Ithaca, SUNY, Utica College at Syracuse, etcetera. Surprisingly enough, I got accepted to them all. Finally, something in my past was paying off in a good day, and it was enough to give me the confidence I needed.

As the acceptance letters began to roll in from other universities that I hadn't previously heard from, something inside of me kept pushing me to get away. Just like I had done in the girls' homes, I wanted to run again. After opening an acceptance letter from Virginia Union University, the desire to leave Buffalo and everyone in it behind strengthened. I hopped on a train and made my way to the nearest Marine Corps Recruiting Office in downtown Buffalo.

I met with a sergeant and told him about my desire to join the reserves. After all, my cousin, Antoine, had joined and was successful in escaping the madness we'd grown up in.

"Unfortunately, there's no reserves for women," the sergeant said, leaning back in his desk chair. He was a black man who looked to be about fifty years old. He seemed to be well built, evidenced by his broad shoulders and protruding chest muscles.

He had given me disappointing news, but I wanted to explore other options. I was determined to get away. This time, however, I didn't want to run to a place called nowhere and end up on the streets or back in prison.

"So what other options do I have?" I asked, folding the brochure I had taken from him.

"Active duty. You can leave right after you finish high school and travel the world."

It sounded good to me. I was impulsive and desperate at the same time.

"Okay. I'll sign up for active duty," I said.

"Wait a minute. Since you're only seventeen, we're going to need parental approval."

"I'm an emancipated minor, sir. I have no parents," I said, hoping he'd not convey another roadblock.

After the formalities were worked out and the appropriate approvals obtained, I started the process of enlisting in the Marine Corps. While I was a bit ambivalent of not having followed the intended path of going to college, I was, nevertheless, content and firm in my decision to join the Marine Corps. I wouldn't have to worry about money, food, or shelter. These things were provided for by the military.

I sliced myself up pretty good that night. The physical pain was numbing in comparison to the emotional pain, which was unbearable. It had been over three weeks since I'd spoken to Charles, and in that time I made a lot of rash decisions that would later have a major impact on my life. I went to bed that night with blood shot eyes and tears pasted to my skin, with my knife under my pillow. The neighborhood I lived in was not, by far, the safest. After finally dozing off, my sleep was abruptly disturbed by a figure hovering over me.

I sprang to my feet and backed myself into a corner. As my eyes focused, I could make the figure out. It was Mark! I broke out in a cold sweat. My hands shook uncontrollably as I tried to shield my face from the knife he was holding.

"What do you want?" I yelled out.

"Who the hell you got those roses from," he asked, pointing to the vase of three-week-old wilted roses given to me by Charles.

"A guy I used to see," I said, leaving out details.

Mark grabbed a handful on the petals and through them at me. "Get your ass dressed. You're coming with me."

I was paralyzed with fear and couldn't move.

"I said, get yo ass dressed, or you gonna find this blade in your back."

This was a very different Mark than the one I'd known. I didn't know how he had found me. I hadn't seen him since the day he kicked me out of make good on his promise to stab me.

"H..how....d...did you find out where I lived?" I said, gliding against the wall over to my closet door.

"Followed you home from school a few days ago."

"How did you get in here?" I followed up with, reaching for shirt in the closet.

"That window," he said, pointing to my bedroom window. "Look, stop asking questions. Just get your shit on and let's roll."

He was still holding the knife in his hand. It looked more like a switchblade than a kitchen knife, but I didn't want to stare. He was already agitated enough. I put the shirt on and was searching for a pair of denim jeans when Mark made the mistake of going to use the bathroom. I jumped out of my bedroom window. I landed down hard on my left ankle, preventing me from taking off running. As I galloped down the driveway, I was blinded by the lights to a vehicle driving up. I tried to hide behind the big bush on the left side of the driveway.

"Tiffany!" a man's voice called out to me.

I stopped in my tracks. It was a familiar voice—it was Charles. As I hurriedly headed toward Charles, Mark stuck his head out of the window and yelled out my name.

"Tiffany!"

I didn't answer.

"Tiffany, I'm gonna kill yo ass!"

"Hurry, hurry," I said, running over to Charles who had coincidentally come over at the right time.

"Who's that?" Charles said, trying to make the figure out in the darkness.

"He's going to kill me! He's going to kill me!" I screamed, galloping past Charles and over to the passenger side of his truck.

By the time Mark made his way down the driveway, Charles was more than prepared to confront him.

"What the hell do you think ya doin'?" he said, his accent thick and strong now.

"F**k you, dude. Tiffany, I said you're coming with me," Mark said, walking over to the truck.

I opened the passenger door, hopped in, and locked the doors.

"I'm going to call the police on ya," Charles said, using his body to block Mark from trying to open the passenger door.

The two made direct eye contact for a few moments, and eventually, Mark acquiesced and walked away into the night. In that instant, something inside released. I broke down.

"Come on," Charles said, as he opened the door and extended his arms to hold me.

I fell into his arms and cried for a good fifteen or so minutes. I couldn't sort through the feelings of hurt and anger I held toward Charles, because in that moment, he was my savior. He provided me the solace I needed to recover from the trauma I had just endured by staying with me the entire night, not trying to have sex with me, but just being there. I decided to have him another chance.

∞ ∞ ∞ ∞

I moved out of that apartment soon after the incident. But the thought of Mark standing over me with the knife haunted me for a good while. It's what started me sleeping with the lights on at night. It didn't, however, keep me from abruptly awakening at night with drenched pajamas.

By mid-spring 1994, I was preparing to graduate and was in the midst of selecting colleges to attend. I started back up with calling home to 920 Lafayette periodically to check on the family. During one such call, Aunt Denise gave me some surprising news.

"Your mother's coming to town."

The news was surreal and rendered me ambivalent momentarily. I'd finally have an opportunity to meet her. I never considered her lost; I always told everyone she abandoned me. The missing part of my identity was coming to visit. Immediately, long-held thoughts and desires raced in my head. *Do I look like her? What drove her to leave me for dead?* I wanted to know what it felt like to be held by her. I wanted to hear her tell me that she loved me. My thoughts went from sentimental to detrimental. I wanted to see her cry and regret ever leaving me in a hellhole. I wanted her to see my scars and feel my pain for a long while. I wanted to know why she never came back for me. I want to know why she failed me and why she never made good on the promises she made in the two Christmas cards she sent, if she had ever event sent them. There were so many holes in my life story that needed to be filled. I suppose I was just growing older and saw things now with the eyes of an adult, instead of a child. There was no overlooking the fact that clearly she made other things priority in her life, and they didn't include me. So taking it all into consideration, I couldn't really be excited about her impending arrival, although I was anxious for it.

"So when is she supposed to be here?" I asked Aunt Denise, nonchalantly.

"In about a week."

"How long is she staying?" I followed up with.

"I dunno, a week or so. She's bringing her husband and your brother with her. I don't know their exact schedules, so I can't be too sure how long they'll be here."

Now, I have to admit. I was excited to learn that I had a brother. There was another extension of me in this world. Someone who was just as innocent as I was. Someone who had had a different life with the woman who birthed us both. So I couldn't wait to meet him and bond with him. That's if my mother hadn't poisoned his mind with ill thoughts of me. By default, however, my meeting with my brother would be delayed because I didn't want Conitra, or any of the others, for that matter, to think I was in a rush to plant my eyes on my mother.

I did not end up seeing my mother until three days after her arrival. I was in school the day she came, and that certainly took priority. But when I arrived at 920 Lafayette, I paused before I rang the doorbell. My stomach performed mini-cartwheels as I stood there waiting for someone to open the door.

I don't remember taking the steps to enter the house, but I, undoubtedly, must have. Conitra, my mother, was sitting off to the left of the living room. She was seated on my grandmother's green plastic-covered sofa. A young boy, who I presumed to be my brother, was in the middle of the floor glued to the TV, which was mounted on top of the black and white console TV that I'd watched growing up. The picture tube had died a few years back, so Grandma Anita replaced it with a new one but never got rid of the old console TV.

When I walked in, they both stared at me; I felt like a monkey on display at the zoo.

"Oh my God! Look at you!" my mother exclaimed, getting up from her seat. "Come give momma a hug," she said, holding her arms out as she walked up to me.

I looked her over quickly. She didn't look down and out. In fact, she looked like any normal woman I could see walking down the street. She wore what appeared to be an engagement ring on her wedding finger. On her right middle finger, she wore a ring with some sort of birthstone in it. I glanced up at her neck and could see the old wound from her having been cut during the attack. But as much as I could find a reason to feel sorry for her, I had plenty more reasons not to. For starters, her emotions didn't seem genuine to me, she acted as if I had gone to the corner store and gotten lost in the process. Her words simply didn't register with me either. Momma? That wasn't who she was to me. Nevertheless, however, I reluctantly honored her request and gave her a mini-hug, if I had to make up a term to describe the gesture. I barely touched her, and there was certainly no attached emotion.

"What's your name?" I said to my little brother, shifting my attention from my mother and the others.

"Russell," he said, looking up at me. He had big, round eyes and was just the epitome of handsome. Like me, he was caramel toned, but unlike me, his hair texture was fine and wavy. We didn't share any obvious physical resemblance.

"Can I get a hug?" I asked, reaching me arms out toward him.

He got up and almost leaped into my arms. There was an instant connection between the two of us. I couldn't explain it, but I felt it immediately.

"So how long are you going to be here?" I asked, diverting my attention back to my mother.

"I'll be here for a minute. Your grandma not doing too well."

"Where is she?" I said, scanning the room.

"In the kitchen," Aunt Denise said, pointing in the direction of the kitchen.

I excused myself from the living room and went into the kitchen to speak with Grandma Anita, something that was more customary as opposed to genuinely desired.

"Hey, Grandma," I said as I entered the kitchen. She looked up and nodded. She was "pulling together a meal," as she called it. This simply meant, she didn't have a pre-designed menu but was going to make dishes of food on the whim. After all, she probably felt the same way I felt about my mother—she didn't deserve a Thanksgiving-like meal in celebration of delayed visit.

"What are you making?" I said, to stir up conversation.

"You know me, Tiff. I'm just pulling a lil somethin' together."

We chuckled because it was one of her infamous sayings, but when it was all said and done, she'd prepare several different tasty dishes for us to grub on.

Silence fell upon us for a few moments. I think we were thinking the same thing, but I dared not venture into the territory. But after a few moments, Grandma Anita broke the silence.

"So what do you think of her?"

"Nothing. I don't think nothing," I said.

"Welp, I can't blame you," Grandma Anita said, opening the oven to retrieve her cornbread muffins. "It's gon' take some time for you to sort your feelings out. But you gon' have to have that talk with her before she leaves," she forecasted.

I knew what that talk meant the minute the words left Grandma Anita's lips. For the first time, however, she appeared to be "on my side".

"I know....I know," I confessed.

"Know what?" my mother said, bursting in on our conversation.

Grandma Anita looked at me and raised her eyebrows, giving me the go ahead. Apparently, she thought it might be a good time to confront my mother about.... *almost everything.*

I lit right in on my mother. "About leaving me!" I yelled. "Why the hell did you leave me!"

Aunt Denise came running into the kitchen. But this wasn't about her; it was about Tiffany and Conitra.

"Tiffany, I was young. I was...I tried. I really tried, but it was hard. I couldn't make it with—"

"You tried? I don't want to hear about how you tried! You should have been here—come hell or high water, you should have been here! How dare you leave me behind! Do you know what I went through—the pain, the sleepless nights? Do you even care?" I said, cutting her off.

"Tiff...you'd never understand," my mother said, glaring at Grandma Anita. I knew what the glare meant, but my current anger was directed toward her, not Grandma Anita. Had she never left me, I would have never suffered the years of abuse at Grandma Anita's hands.

"Please don't call me Tiff....My name is Tiffany. The name 'Tiff' is reserved for people who've been there for me, like Granddad Carlos, your father, remember him?" I said, a direct jab at her for not even showing up at his funeral.

"You'd never understand," she mumbled under her breath.

I let it go, and walked out of the kitchen. I stopped in the living room and said good-bye to Robert.

"I'll be back and we can hang out some," I promised.

"Cool!" he said, probably excited knowing he'd get out the house to go out on excursions.

∞ ∞ ∞ ∞

Charles came over to be with me that night. My emotions were on ten. But as always, Charles had a way of comforting me and getting me to deescalate my raging emotions.

"You know, you've long to meet your mother...to see who she actually is. And face it, you're probably never going to have the chummy-chum relationship with her. But give her a chance. At least get the answers you've always wanted."

"But she just seemed like it was nothing to her, like she had done nothing wrong," I said, lifting my head from his lap.

"If you keep barking at her, she's going to shut down for good. Look, you've told me what you went through with your grandmother. Who's to say she didn't go through the same thing?"

Actually, Charles had made some excellent points. Perhaps he was right and my barking at my mother was going to drive her away. I still had some questions for her, like where was my father. So in that moment, I purposed that I would lay off her as far as the attacks were concerned and would try to see past my own pain and give Conitra, my mother, a chance.

∞ ∞ ∞ ∞

I went back over to 920 Lafayette a few days later, for the sole purpose of spending some time with my mother, to try to get to know her. She was sitting on the front porch when I walked up to the house.

"Hey, how's it going?" she said, getting up from her chair.

"Good," I said, walking up the porch steps. I didn't how to pretend to be something that I wasn't—warm and friendly. I gave her another fake hug and sat down in the chair across from the chair she had been sitting in.

"I'd like to come over to see your place before you leave," she said, sitting back down in the chair.

I was a bit taken aback by her comment. She seemed like she wanted to get too close to me. I didn't have much, but my little apartment was my safe haven, and I didn't want anyone trespassing.

"Okay," I lied. I had no intention on bring her to my apartment.

"I want to see your color scheme and set up so I can buy you a housewarming gift."

"Oh okay," I said, trying to sound amicable.

Erie silence fell upon us. I cut it with a burning question. "Who's my dad?"

She lowered her head. "I'm not sure," she mumbled.

I wanted more from her, though. I wanted to hear her tell me the truth about her irresponsibility. However, she sat in denial, and instead, she would not say anymore, which simply confirmed that she, too, had become a master at suppressing the deep emotions that dug up deep wounds.

"You know, Peter, Russell, and I are going to Disneyland soon. It would be nice if you could join us." Peter was her boyfriend who, for whatever reason, didn't accompany my mother and brother on the trip.

I wasn't sure if it was a genuine invite or just a tactic to change the subject to something interesting and alluring.

"I dunno. I have a lot going on. I'm going to school, you know. And I'm also about to go to the Marines," I bragged. I wanted her to know I was going to make something of myself anyway. I wanted her to be envious and jealous of me, like I was of all the other kids that lived normal lives with a mother and father at home.

"Just let me know then. I'd love to have to join us."

"Well, like I said, I have a lot going on, so I can't make that commitment at this very moment. I'll have to see."

"That's good enough for me," she said with a half-cracked smile.

∞ ∞ ∞ ∞

I supposed that we had made some progress by the time my mother went back to Seattle. I was a little saddened to see them go. I was going to miss my brother more than anything. I ended up escorting them to the Amtrak station to ensure that they got off safely. I waved good-bye as they boarded. Once they were out of sight, I went my separate way. I didn't know exactly how I felt about the whole visit, but it was now over, and I exhaled.

∞ ∞ ∞ ∞

I fell behind on my bills, and, with no money, I had to move out of my apartment. I decided not to call upon the Masons to help me. Although their home was always open to me, I couldn't live with the thought of my shortcomings having disappointed them. Although Charles and I had grown closer and he had actually invited me to live with him during this time, I declined his offer. I had no desire to be like the other women in my family by falling into co-dependency and emotional traps with men. I really only had one option—moving back to 920 Lafayette. Despite the overall dysfunction, it was still my home, and I was still family. I was older at that point, and I knew how to stand up for myself. So the thought of Grandma Anita or Aunt Denise laying a hand on me didn't deter me.

I came mentally prepared; I told myself that if she did hit me, I would sure enough fight back this time. Mentally, I was much tougher than when I had last lived there. The streets had taught me a lot.

I planned out what I would say before I even dialed the number from the local payphone.

"Hey, Aunt Denise."

"I've been trying to reach you, but your phone is disconnected."

"Yeah, it got disconnected," I said embarrassingly.

"Well, you know Mama's been in and out of the hospital lately. That's what I was tryna call to tell you."

I was embarrassed for not having communicated since my mother went back to Seattle. Quitting my job behind Charles was definitely not the right thing to have done. Now, I had to put my tail between my legs and go back to the place I vowed never to return.

"How is she?

"She has her good days and bad days. Between the Alzheimer's, diabetes, and heart failure all going on at the same time, it's a wonder she's still alive." Aunt Denise said, in between coughs. She had asthma and still smoked, so she often coughed a lot.

"She at Buffalo General or County?" I asked. But Aunt Denise couldn't hear me due to the sound of a passing police siren.

"Where are you, outside?"

"Yeah. I'm using a payphone. I lost my place."

"How'd you do that?"

"I lost my job," I lied.

"What are you going to do, Tiffany? You know if ain't safe to be out there on the streets."

"I was going to ask grandma if I could come back there until I got up on my feet."

"Well, you can definitely come on home. I only ask that you help out around the house...laundry, cooking, dishes, and I stuff like that.

"I have food stamps, so I can help buy food in the house, too," I volunteered.

"That's cool. When you coming?"

"Soon as I can get a few things together and have Charles bring me over there. But I don't need to be there all that long. I got accepted in the EOP (short for, Equal Opportunity Program) at Canisius College, and I'll be there a week after school is out. And I also went to see a recruiter at the Marine Corps. I'm slated to leave for there in November."

"That's cool," Aunt Denise congratulated. I'm not sure she was truly happy for me, but "that's cool" was about the best she could offer me. The Duson women were not warm people at all.

So Aunt Denise and I had a deal. I called Charles and told him about the plans I'd just made, and he sprung right into action. He gathered up a few of his guy friends, and they helped me move out of my apartment back to 920 Lafayette that night.

It felt a little weird moving back into the room that held so many haunting memories of my childhood. It seemed like very little had changed in the house, except for the two new Cockatiels Aunt Denise owned. Aunt Denise literally lived in the same room that she'd been in when I was a kid. Her addiction habits were out of control. She drank all night and slept all day, and she was still dependent on her boyfriend Jimmy to buy her cigarettes, play her lotto numbers, bills, and supply her liquor, marijuana, and cocaine on the regular.

∞ ∞ ∞ ∞

The day of my high school graduation was a happy day for me. I was dreaming in living color. I had become close friends with a girl by the name of Jennifer Steele. She and I bonded during the last months of school. We bought matching outfits to wear under our gowns, had our hair done by her cousin, April, who was a hairstylist, and celebrated like true champs that day.

None of my family members showed up at graduation, as they were off on their own individual missions. Aunt Theresa who had abused and robbed Grandma Anita blind before her hospitalization was rumored to be homeless and completely strung out on cocaine. Aunt Denise said that she last seen prostituting on the Genesee strip somewhere. Uncle Dennis was diagnosed with HIV and had disappeared, and for whatever reason, Aunt Denise didn't show up either. But I had made it, and nobody was going to take that joy and accomplishment away from me!

As I walked across the stage that day, my classmates began to sing the Looney Toons' anthem in unison. It was an inside joke, having always been referred to as "Tweety Bird"—I had a big head and little body. But all in all, June 24, 1994, was a great day for me, and I was looking forward to starting summer school at Canisius the following Monday.

Everyone thought I was crazy for going to college in the summer and not taking the summer off. In my mind, it wasn't like I ever had a summer, so it didn't matter. Things were beginning to look good for me, and I was happy that I had not fallen victim to the grim statistics as nearly everyone had expected. The moment was joyous for me, even though I was the only one celebrating my achievement. But rightfully so because I had earned it and had become the first in my immediate family to graduate from high school, and to add icing to the cake, was the first to go on to college. I was determined to make an extraordinary impact and be a trailblazer! I had overcome obstacles since I exited my mother's womb—obstacles of income and resources, education, love, support, and encouragement. I had finally begun to defy the odds. I knew there was a fire in me, and I was determined to let it spread!

Then, my menstrual cycle was late!

"Rain brings Reign"

It frees up the hope bound within
the seed
Reaching those places untouchable
by human hands
Our most essential element for
existence...Water
For within our soiled lives, our dirty
deeds and our questionable past
There is something within them that
causes us to increase strength
Something that expands our area...and
extends our length

And it is not to be seen with the
naked eye
You can't sit in the garden...and watch
growth take place
It is a private happening...unfolding
at a more intimate pace

Within the muck and mire is a nutrient
that causes us to grow
We get stronger when we rise above
the hurt
No pain, no gain...No growth means
no dirt

And then the rain comes and unlocks
us from our jail
It unleashes the potential that we
have stored
What once was our ceiling...now
becomes our floor

We rise above former vision...
and we see better from this height
We now have a foundation of support...
whether self, friend, parent or spouse
The lessons we learned in the basement...
are what we teach in the penthouse

And our roots have grown strong...
because they had to go deeper than
our situations
Patience is ours...and a wealth
of experience to turn to
We can handle so much more now...look
at all that we've already been through

God takes the negative things that we
daily pray to be rid of
And uses them to create a beautiful
tapestry...albeit colored with pain
Because He knows that once He brings the
water...we have no choice but to Reign.

CHAPTER NINE

Killing the Curse

L iving with Aunt Denise didn't turn out to be such a bad experience. I only had ten days before it was time to move on campus, and I was very excited. Charles and I were still together and had recently celebrated our two-year anniversary. But I was also plagued with worry over my missed menstrual period. Charles and I discussed the fact that I could be pregnant. I was adamant about not wanting children at that stage in my life. My mother had gotten pregnant around the same age, and I didn't want to repeat the cycle.

I went to Rite-Aid pharmacy and purchased a pregnancy test. Charles and I went back to his place to take it.

"Don't be nervous," Charles consoled, having noticed my hands trembling as I pried open the test box.

I read the directions quickly, and peed on the test stick as directed. Charles and I waited for the three minutes to pass, looking periodically at the stick to see if there was any change of color in the test window. Slowly but surely, a pink line appeared in the test window indicating a positive test result. My heart sank.

I stayed at Charles's apartment that night. We discussed next steps as if we were making strategic business plans. I had to push past my emotions, if I was going to be successful in going through with the abortion. So the last week in June, Charles and I went to an abortion clinic on Main Street. We were met by a group of protestors who tried to convince me to pursue another route, whether it meant keeping the child and rearing him or her or giving the baby up for adoption. I could name quite a few people who had gotten pregnant too soon, and their lives hadn't turned out too well. Pregnancy, to me, meant being stuck in the projects, poor, and destitute. I didn't wait for Charles to open the entrance door, I opened it myself and went inside to do what I'd come there to do.

∞ ∞ ∞ ∞

On July 1, 1994, I finally took a trip to Erie County Medical Center to see Grandma Anita. She had been moved there because it had a rehabilitation floor and Buffalo General didn't. It was the first time I'd seen her since learning that she had become very ill.

Charles took me up to the hospital. Her floor reeked of urine and other foul smells. The air was stale, the rooms and décor all blended in, and the food was enough to give you indigestion by just looking at it. Erie County Medical Center was viewed as a place where people went to die. If you wanted to increase your odds of survival, you'd be better off going to Buffalo General. But by this time, Grandma Anita had been in County for some time. She'd lost over 120 pounds, and she lay there completely helpless. She looked nothing like I remembered her. It was ironic that the woman who was once a powerhouse and could strike fear in your spirit by the mere sound of her voice, was now lame, not in her right mind, and afflicted by deteriorating health, including a failing heart. She lay in that bed clinging to life without much fight in her.

I walked in her room and gazed at her. She was staring at the TV, not watching really, just more so in a semi-conscious daze. I fought back the tears, initially. Holding onto remnants of my past in that moment, I didn't want to cry for her, but I was overwhelmed with sadness. I called out to her.

"Grandma."

She turned her head slightly in my direction and made eye contact.

We had some small talk, most of which was unfruitful and unproductive due to the memory lapses caused by her Alzheimer's. But in between the episodic memory

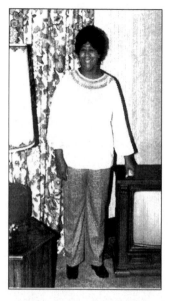

lapses, Grandma Anita did have the wherewithal to ask for a Snickers candy bar. I knew the hospital staff were probably against her having one, but I saw no harm in fulfilling her request. After all, she was now living and dying in her own personal hell, at the same time. So before I left, I went down the hall to the vending machine and bought a Snickers candy bar. She was sound asleep by the time I walked back into her room. I slid the candy under her pillow, kissed her on the forehead, and left her peaceful with her morphine drip.

∞ ∞ ∞ ∞

The Duson family was notorious for throwing large barbeques. Family, friends, and neighbors would make it their business to come by to eat, drink, and be merry. I had mastered Anita's recipe for barbeque sauce, incorporating with my own twist, of course. We hadn't all been together just to have a good time in God knows how long. But we enjoyed the day shooting off firecrackers, wetting one another up with water guns, and enjoying good food and laughs. I hadn't had this much fun with my blood family probably since I was five or six years old. I had purposed that I wouldn't go down memory lane with the traumatic things of the past, so I just relished in the moment.

I left the barbeque a little early so Charles and I could stop by the Masons. I thought it was a good time for them to meet Charles, since our relationship had been going strong for more than two years. Papa made his usual speech about God, love, and not hurting his daughter. He winked at me after their talk had come to an end. I guess he approved. Mama Mason, on the other hand, seemed to like Charles right off the bat. She used her female intuition as a barometer of whether she liked a person or not. I wouldn't outright say it, but her willingness to engage in more than five minutes of conversation let me know that Charles was good in her book as well. Karisma was an easy sell because she tended to like good-looking men, period, and Charles was very good looking.

I left the Masons with plates of food and some dessert, and Charles and I headed back to my dorm. I was some tired that one day.

∞ ∞ ∞ ∞

I'm guessing it was somewhere between two and three o'clock in the morning when my dorm telephone rang. Although it was soft, I caught the voice right away. It was Aunt Denise.

"Are you up?"

"Yes," I said sitting up in the bed.

"The police just left the house—". She paused.

What happened? I wondered.

"Mama died tonight."

I don't readily recall what she said next. My hearing left me for a few seconds and the room went dark. I slid out of the bed and stood motionless—waiting.

"Tiffany? Did you hear me?" Aunt Denise asked.

I hadn't heard what she had said and therefore couldn't answer her.

"I didn't hear you," I said, my hearing seemingly having been restored.

"You wanna call and let Conitra....I mean, your mother know?" she repeated.

"Nah, I don't think I can handle doing that. Just call her yourself. I just don't think I can handle doing that," I said.

After a moment of hesitation, she said, "Okay."

"If you need me to help with anything, just let me know. I'll stop by in a couple of days to see how things are going."

"All right. I'll call you."

I didn't have a burning desire to run to be by Aunt Denise's side, and neither did she have the desire to come be beside mine. That's how we Duson women were fashioned. The wicked witch was dead, and I didn't know how I felt about it. To me, Grandma Anita was an incurable cancer. She was contagious in the sense that she afflicted everyone she touched. For years, everyone had been subjected to her anger, bitterness, and pain. Therefore, a true, sincere feeling of remorse was non-existent. As a matter of fact, news of her death didn't garner much of a reaction at all from anyone, including neighbors and family friends.

I made good on my promise to stop by a few days later to check on Aunt Denise and her progress with making the funeral arrangements. But when asked if I would be in attendance at the funeral, I gave my sincere apologies. "I'm sorry, I have class," I said as I walked down the porch steps of 920 Lafayette Street and headed back to my dorm.

As I walked down Main Street to my Calculus class the following Tuesday, I caught a glimpse of Grandma Anita's funeral procession. I stopped and had a personal moment of silence. I said my final good-bye, in my own way and in my own style, as the procession rolled out of view. I never knew or did ask where she was buried. I didn't want any other memories than those that she had left me with. I loved her, but I hated her.

I saw the 4th of July that year as a significant day in my history. It was my personal Independence Day from the ties that bound me. The scars were deep, but I believed I was now well on my way to freedom and recovery.

She Speaks

CHAPTER TEN

The Few were Proud

W hen September 1994 rolled around, and the fall semester of regular classes at Canisius began, I quickly discovered just how challenging college was in comparison to high school, which had been a cakewalk for me. There was more reading, loads of writing, and tons of thinking, to sum it up. I was on a partial scholarship and was receiving financial aid. I found out during the first week of classes that my financial aid was not enough to cover all of my expenses, and dorm living was eating up over five thousand dollars of my aid. To remedy the problem, a select group of friends and I decided to move off campus. We figured that we'd collect the balance of our money and make out better in an apartment, so we packed up and moved about two blocks from the school campus.

I had lived with people before, so moving in with the girls didn't pose a challenge for me. My schemes and antics, however, ended up being true nightmares for my roommates. I spent more time partying than I did studying, and it was definitely a recipe for disaster. Before I realized it, I was losing focus and becoming increasingly reckless, leaving me in a position to lose everything, including my scholarship. I was, however, still enlisted in the Marine Corps Recruit Program and had been officially sworn in, solidifying my commitment to Uncle Sam. It was mid-September, and, having already requested to move my ship date back, I was unsure of what I was going to do. My bills were piling, tuition costs had escalated, and my grades had begun to decline.

Charles had no idea about the mess I had gotten myself into, but because I knew I had to get out of Buffalo real fast, I concocted a lie.

"I think I'm going to take my mother up on her offer," I said one day.

"You sure about that?" Charles asked, quizzically.

"Yeah, why not."

"What about school?"

"I can always go back. I've been doing thing the untraditional way all my life, so I can get my education in the same manner," I said, trying to convince myself more so than Charles.

"Well, if you look at it that way, then, you're right," he said, growing quiet immediately afterward.

"What's wrong?" I asked, not sure of what he was actually thinking.

"I guess if we're going to be together, I'm going to have to move out to Seattle after I finish school."

I didn't answer. I couldn't be sure where I would end up, so I definitely didn't want to encourage Charles to make future plans.

"Did you talk to your parents?" he followed up with, referring to Mama and Papa Mason.

"No, not yet. Papa's gonna have a problem with it, I can tell you that now. Mama, I'm not so sure," I answered.

Charles didn't give me a hard time about my decision to drop out of college. He knew me well. So in the back of his mind, I think he knew something else was going on, but he didn't probe any further.

∞ ∞ ∞ ∞

I dropped out of college in late September and opted to take the credit card that I had applied for earlier that month and purchase a one-way ticket to Seattle.

I spent three long days on a greyhound bus riding across the country, sleeping at rest stops, eating at scheduled connection cities, and viewing mountains, valleys, and other eye-catching scenery along the way. I was somewhat ambivalent about moving somewhere new. I had grown up in Buffalo all my life, and was eager to breathe in a different type of air. I only prayed that my journey was worth it.

I arrived in Seattle on a Monday evening. My mother had sent Peter to meet me at the bus station.

"He's Asian," my mother had told me. So I knew to look for an Asian man when I stepped off the bus.

Peter and I spotted one another almost immediately. I gave him a once over. I couldn't see the connection between him and my mom at all. Peter stood barely five feet tall, had a pudgy waistline and jet-black hair. His English was poor and his mannerisms were not like anything I was used to.

"All you bags?" he asked in his chopped up version of the English language.

"Yep, all my bags," I said, pulling the last of my luggage from the bottom storage area of the bus.

Peter grabbed all three of my bags. "I park car down there," he said, leaning his head in the direction of where he had parked their car.

I guess my mom had instructed Peter to "lay down the law" with me when he picked me up, because he gave me the rundown of the dos and don'ts nearly our entire ride home.

"You stay in room with Rus-sal," he said, mispronouncing Russell's name.

I wasn't too bothered by having to share a room with Russell because he was cool. Of course I'd rather have my own room, but my mother, Peter, and Russell were living the life that accommodated their needs. So I had to make the best of what was being offered to me.

I nodded. "So where are you from?" I asked Peter, changing the subject.

"Korea," he said proudly.

"What's Seattle really like?" I was hoping to get some sense of Seattle's social environment. The last thing I wanted to do was sit in the house like a maid and find chores to do. I knew it didn't take much for me to become bored, so I wanted to have some idea of just what I could get into.

"And you got to get job," he added.

I guess my mother was going to make sure my "indefinite" stay wasn't going to cost her too much money. It wasn't like she had spent tons of money on me in the past, so for her to demand that I get a job straight out the gate was an immediate turnoff to me.

"Look, I'mma need a few days to feel my way around before I start looking for a job. I might not even be staying," I snapped.

Peter nodded. I took his nod for agreement and said nothing further. I was quiet the remainder of the ride.

∞ ∞ ∞ ∞

They lived in a modest, white ranch-style house with burgundy shutters. The yard was neatly and beautifully manicured with adorning flowers and bushes clustered around the house and its medium-sized driveway. *Conitra has certainly carved herself out a nice little life far away in Seattle,* I thought, looking around.

"Nice yard," I said.

"You mother like nice things," Peter said as he pulled my luggage up the driveway.

"I can help you with the bags," I offered.

"No....got it," he said between breaths as he hiked up the driveway.

The inside of the house didn't have any sparks or majestic highlights to it, but it matched the outside décor, white kitchen cabinets with burgundy accents. The living room was styled with contemporary furnishings, a cream leather sofa, loveseat, and chair and matching burgundy ornaments throughout. A large television sat in the far left corner of the room.

"Have seat. I bring these to you room," Peter said, heading to the room I would be sharing with Russell.

I sat down on the loveseat, and grabbed the remote control. I flashed past several channels before I found a program I was interested in watching—The Oprah Winfrey Show. Peter came back to the living room after putting my bags in the room and gave me a brief rundown on where I could find this or that in the house, in his attempt to make me feel at home. The truth was, however, I was a stranger to my mother on both physical and psychological levels, and living in the same house with her wasn't going to change it anytime soon. But

I knew he was only doing what he thought to be hospitable, so I acknowledged his effort.

"Thank you," I said, reverting my attention back to the show.

∞ ∞ ∞ ∞

The daily routine was pretty simple and one I had to get used to. The house was pretty empty and quiet during the day. Peter was a Janitorial Supervisor, so with the exception of the day he picked me up at the bus station, he left early in the morning and didn't return home until very late at night. When he did come home, he would get something to eat and stay locked in his and my mother's bedroom. He was extremely antisocial, and I got the impression that he really didn't care for my brother or me. Russell was in school most of the day, and my mother worked the private nurse shift four days a week at the home of some rich elderly couple. Tired from the shift, she'd sleep for most of the day on her first day off.

∞ ∞ ∞ ∞

I did the entire tourist thing for my first two weeks, learning my way around the hilly territory in due time. Once I finished touring the area, I became bored. With limited outlets, I spent a great deal of my time monitoring Russell's progress in school and preparing meals for the family. Peter ate separate meals altogether and didn't indulge in anything I cooked.

I started looking for a job during the third week of my stay and ended up getting a job in sales, going door-to-door selling promotional packages. It paid on commission. By the end of each day, I had walked several miles, and my feet hurt badly. I kept the job for nearly two weeks before I quit and landed a gig with a multilevel marketing company called Equinox. I was sold on their products, not to mention the fact that they had a product that was guaranteed to help my mom quit smoking, as well as a showerhead that filtered harmful particles out of your water. I was excited about the purported effectiveness of the products, and I worked hard to get sales. But a few weeks later, my zeal waned, and I realized that I had more products than I could push. I gave up the idea of pyramid schemes and direct sales altogether.

Even though I had no clue what I would do next, I did know what I wasn't going to do—the Marines. I had been running from reporting for duty since the date I signed up. But I also knew that if I didn't make some sort of communicative effort, they'd come looking for me. So I called one day.

"Where are you, Miss Duson?" my recruiter, MSgt. Taylor asked. He had grown very impatient with me but was still willing to work with me before giving up and putting in notice that I was AWOL.

"Seattle," I said.

"You do know that you signed a contract, don't you?" he said, his way of reminding me of my obligation and the Marines' right to enforce it.

"Yeah, I know," answered nonchalantly.

"I'm really trying to work with you, but I can only do so much."

I held the phone and didn't readily respond.

"But I'll tell you what. I can push your ship date back again."

"I can't get out of the contract?"

"I'm afraid not. Like I said, I can push your ship date back, but that's about all I can do," he said emphatically.

"Okay. I'll call you back," I said but had no intentions on doing.

∞ ∞ ∞ ∞

By early November, my living situation had become a little testy. I missed being in school and had gone to the University of Washington to just hang out on the campus one particular afternoon. When I came home Peter and I got into it.

"Eww, what's that horrible smell?" I said, upon walking into the kitchen.

Peter was sitting at the kitchen table fiddling with his work pager. "That smell is my dinner, and if you don't like the smell, you can get the hell out," he said rolling his eyes and sucking his teeth.

One thing I noticed right away was that Peter's English sounded perfect when he told someone off. Usually, it's the other way around; the native language or accent becomes dominant when under tension. I stood stunned for a moment, but after the initial shock wore off, I went in on Peter.

"Who the hell do you think you're talking to? You must got me mixed up with Conitra. I ain't no Conitra!" I snapped.

"You're a nasty little freeloader, that's who you are. And you're rude and offensive!" he snapped back.

"I ain't no damn freeloader either, you bastard. I cook, clean, and do all kinds of stuff around here. You must got me twisted with your lazy azz," I retaliated.

"You niggers all alike—lazy," he mumbled as he got up to walk out.

"Did you just call me a nigger?" I said, walking up on him. He didn't know, but I had grown up in the streets, and I was only afraid of a few people, but Peter sure wasn't one of them.

"You heard me," he said, staring me in the eye.

I stepped back, grabbed a pile of dishes and other kitchen utensils that were sitting in the drainer on the counter and hurled them at him, one by one.

"You get the f**k out!" he yelled. "Get the f**k out!"

"No, you get the f**k out!" I yelled back. "It's my mother's house, too, and I ain't gotta go nowhere," I added, steady hurling things at him.

"We'll see about that," he said, catching the spatula with his hands and hurling it back at me.

I ducked and then smiled at him. I knew that burned him up on the inside. He was a male and I, a female. So all it would have taken was for me to call 9-1-1 and report the incident, and he would have been guaranteed a ride downtown with the POPO (slang for police). He finally gave up and stormed to his room, slamming the door behind him.

∞ ∞ ∞ ∞

If I had the remote thought that my mother would be impartial about the tiff Peter and I had, I was more than slightly delusional. When she heard what had transpired, she barged into my room and woke me up.

"Get up, Tiffany. Get the hell up!"

"Huh?" I said, groggily. I knew why she was there.

"Come out in the hallway," she said, not wanting to wake Russell.

I got out of the bed, slid my feet in my worn-down grey slippers I had received from Charles a few Christmases back, and followed my mother into the hallway.

I quickly learned that she wasn't interested in hearing anything I had to say. But she made her wishes very clear—leave. Just like that, I was being kicked out with no place to go. My impending homeless status was the least of my mother's concerns—keeping her man and her fabricated little lifestyle intact took precedence.

"Why am I not surprised that you'd take his side? You're a piss-poor mother!" I shouted.

"I'll be that, but you need to get up out my house, lil' heifer," she shouted back.

It took a few moments for my last comment to sink in, and when it did, she reached for the bat she had undoubtedly had in store for the confrontation and went to swinging.

Trying to dodge the blows, I ran back into the room, closed and locked the door, grabbed what I could, and fled on foot. I hitch-hiked a ride as close to the bus station that I could get. The driver, an older white woman, let me out six blocks away and I walked the rest of the way. I tried to purchase a one-way ticket back to Buffalo but discovered that my credit card had reached the credit card limit. My pride wouldn't allow me to call Charles. He would have done something to get me back to Buffalo, but I was tired of getting into jams and having to call him to bail me out. My only alternative was to call Visa and request an emergency limit increase. I did, and surprisingly, Visa gave me a temporary limit increase. I purchased the ticket and took the next scheduled bus back to the East Coast.

∞ ∞ ∞ ∞

During one of the extended connection stops, I went to the payphone and called my recruiter. I told him that I was on my way back to Buffalo but had nowhere to stay. God gave me favor with this man, because he didn't give me a hard time. In fact, he simply made arrangements for me to stay on board an Air Force base in

Niagara Falls until the date I was set to ship out to the Marine Corps boot camp.

I called Charles, too. The conversation was a bit awkward, the latter half, particularly. It was a conversation that had to take place, nonetheless. I got the feeling that Charles was feeling some kinda way when I asked him how he felt about me leaving. His response was somewhat generic and cliché-ish.

"I mean, you have to do what you have to do," he said.

"So your girlfriend is going to the military and will be gone for who knows how long, and the best you can do is say, 'I gotta do what I gotta do?'" I said, slightly misquoting him.

"I just think it'll be good for you, that's all. It offers money and stability...and you need both."

I know he meant well, but his comment stung. "So you think I should go?" I said with a little bit of an attitude. In all actuality, my fragile ego wanted him to beg me to stay. I had been rejected time and time again, and most recently, by my mother once again. I just wanted to know that someone cared enough to want me to stay with them.

"Tiffany, you know I hate to see you go. I love you—"

I didn't hear anything else he said. I was stuck on I love you. I hadn't heard those words in a while, and it felt good; it lessened the sting of his previous comment.

We wrapped up the conversation with talk about our next month's plans, since Christmas was approaching. I'd be at boot camp celebrating the holiday with my military family, whoever they were. Charles, on the other hand, was slated to graduate from college and would be moving back to Miami to be close to his mother soon afterward. Learning this, I became happy that I was leaving—I wasn't so sure that Charles had long-term plans for me.

∞ ∞ ∞ ∞

I arrived back in New York on November 21, 1994. MSgt. Solomon Taylor met me at the bus station and escorted me to the base that would become my home for the next three days. A central point of my life story was set to begin.

For the three days leading up to my departure for boot camp, MSgt Solomon took me under his wing. He transformed me from an extreme makeover candidate who was homeless into something akin to America's Next Top Model. He put me up in palace-like surroundings, bought me new clothes, paid for a new hairdo, saw that I slept in a bed on clean sheets, and saw to it that I had plenty of food to eat. I left Buffalo late in the afternoon on November 24, 1994, and arrived in South Carolina at 8:35 that evening. It was the first time I had ever flown on an airplane.

I was greeted by uniformed officers as I deboarded the plane. Next, I was escorted to a private room where I remained for four hours until a shuttle arrived to transport me and my fellow recruits to the Island. Once the shuttle had arrived, the recruits were ordered to board the bus. They drove us to the island in the dark of the night. This was done purposely so we wouldn't know where we were or how we got there.

Once I stepped foot on Parris Island, I knew I was trapped. I stood stoically as the woman, whose name was Sgt. Jameson, gave immediate orders. I took in my surroundings, watching the faces of my fellow recruits, and listening to the sound of crickets and other night-time critters in between the verbal demands given by Sgt. Jameson. It became convincingly evident to me at that point that there were only two ways off the island—quit or graduate! It was time for me to become a woman.

Three days later, we met the real deal—our platoon drill instructors. It was G.I. Jane times three, and I quickly discovered that I was not in Kansas anymore, Toto was nowhere to be found, and I could not click my ruby-red slippers and go anywhere. The only thing I could do was spit shine my combat boots and remain in compliance with uniform standards.

Over the next twelve weeks, I endured more physical and mental challenges. Since I had been accustomed to yelling, screaming, cursing, and not being called by my legal name, I wasn't as fazed by the mental challenges as the other female recruits were. Because of my so-called "hardness", I became known for being a wise-cracking, rebellious recruit who blatantly showed no respect for authority. I laughed at everything, even if it was not funny. The physical challenge was a different story, though. I stood a measly five-foot-six, weighing in at one hundred and fifteen pounds. I had no stamina, no gumption, and no get-up-and-go. "The Diva" that initially stepped off that bus onto Parris Island had disappeared. There was nothing glamorous about being on the island, but I had to stay—I had no home to go to. I learned to do what the drill instructors had taught us to do early on, and that was to "suck it up" and press harder.

∞ ∞ ∞ ∞

On February 24, 1995, I proudly marched across the parade deck and graduated from boot camp with Platoon 4040. I had ten days of leave before having to report to my next duty station for formal job training. I decided to make a surprise visit home to see my foster parents in Buffalo. I hadn't told them that I'd left Buffalo or that I'd enlisted in the Corps. To the best of their knowledge, I was in college.

My trip to Buffalo was pretty uneventful. The Masons were doing well and were surprised, yet happy, that I had taken the route and gone to the military. Before I left, I presented my parents with a bumper sticker that read, "My Daughter is a United

States Marine." I did not visit 920 Lafayette, or any of the Dusons, for that matter. My journey into freedom and independence was going pretty smooth, with the exception of a few bumps, and I wanted it to stay that way. I took the remainder of my leave to fly to Miami to visit Charles, who, by this time, had graduated college and moved back home to be near his mother as he had previously indicated.

The following March, I reported to the School of Electrical Engineering at Court House Bay, in Jacksonville, N.C. The social and behavioral environment at the school was largely fashioned by the Marine Corps' long held Credo, which was that students were prohibited from fraternizing with permanent staff on the base. You weren't supposed to look, and you certainly weren't supposed to touch. But the Credo went out the window when I locked eyes with a 6'3", gorgeous hunk of a man of mixed-race and Capeverdian descent. His name was Jonathon DeGrassi, and he hailed from Boston, Massachusetts. Call it love or lust, there was something there almost immediately, and neither of us wanted to fight it. The relationship with Charles had dissipated shortly after my visit that past February, so there was nothing keeping me from moving full speed ahead with Jonathan, and *that*, I did.

Jonathan and I did a lot of sneaking around—climbing in and out of windows and using unauthorized vehicles and barrack locations—to be with one another and have lots and lots of hot, steamy sex. Two months into our relationship, Jonathan proposed. I accepted without hesitation, consummating our engagement. We were both caught up in the whirlwind, not knowing whether it was a true love connection or just lust because of the good sex. On the surface, Jonathan appeared to be the ideal catch, everything a woman could ever want—handsome, protective, a provider, strong-minded—qualities that I wasn't exposed to often growing up. Feelings of euphoria, however, were soon replaced with feelings of fear, insecurity, jealousy, and anger. I had been accused of sleeping around with other men, including Jonathan's roommate, Wendell, who was only a shoulder for me to cry on when Jonathan and I were having our issues. Jonathan and I would break up, get back together, and break up again. I gave him his ring back several times. But, like battered and abused women, I took him back an equal number of times. But I finally realized that the cycle would continue to repeat, and the relationship wasn't going anywhere. So in late June 1995, after suffering so much of Jonathan's abuse, which was mostly verbal, I decided to make our separation permanent. I called the engagement off, and cut him out of my life—or so I thought.

The demise of Jonathan and my relationship quickly became water cooler gossip that spread like wildfire straight to my company commander. Being involved with Jonathan was in total defiance of the Marine Corps

Rules and Regulations. In their view, I had violated the Credo, violated the Corps, violated myself, and because of it, I was subsequently court-marshaled and lost a stripe. Shortly thereafter, I was given orders to Iwakuni, Japan for twelve months. The pressure was definitely building. I viewed the orders as punishment for the violation, and I was angry. I wanted someone to blame, but each time I looked in the mirror, I saw only one person—me.

I arose the next morning for physical fitness formation at 7:00 am for our scheduled run. I fell right into the ranks and ran three miles. During the final stretch of the run, I became dizzy and nauseated. I assumed my malady was a result of the shots I'd received in preparation for my overseas deployment and thought nothing more of it. It wasn't long before the error in my self-diagnosis was revealed.

Miner's Mouthful

Did....dig....dig....dig!!!!
Deeper....get it down deeper!!
Bury it until it can never be found
Never mind the sweat, blood and tears
Hide this secret deep inside...ignore
it for years
Act like it never happened
Yeah...that's it...just walk normal...no one
will know
Fix your skirt...wash your face...pray the
bloodstains will not show
Or the silent whispers might be
overheard
So bite down hard...never mention
a word
Clench your teeth the same way you
clenched your legs
Shut your emotions down like you shut
your mouth

Now gulp down the hope that it will be
over soon
The notion that someone will come and
rescue you
Get used to what was "crazy"...now
becoming your everyday

What was unbelievable has become
your core belief
Mercy is something that you will
never see
The new morning will bring no relief
So dig....damn you!
Dig like your life depended on it
Like your sanity hinged on the depth
of the hole
Bury as much as you can fit into this void
And digest the dirt you remove so that no
evidence shows
No one notices brown teeth anymore
So don't worry....there's no time for you
to ponder and wallow
Just dig....dig....dig until it's as deep
as the pain
And then...grab a mirror...and swallow

He Speaks

She Speaks

CHAPTER ELEVEN

April Fools...

July 4, 1995, Courthouse Bay (Camp Lejeune), NC, I was making final preparations to leave the South. Jonathon and I hadn't spoken in a while. Mother Nature hadn't visited, which was unusual for me because I had been on schedule for as long as I could remember. I purchased a pregnancy test from the store on base. I hurried back to my barrack and took the test. It revealed what I feared—I was pregnant with Jonathon's child.

Due to the status our relationship, it was in the dumps or nonexistent altogether, I decided not to tell Jonathan just yet. In fact, I decided to keep my pregnancy a secret, at least for the time being. If my company commander found out, it would essentially mean no transfer overseas.

Being pregnant in the military, however, did carry certain benefits. With a doctor's note confirming pregnancy, a pregnant woman could receive base housing, extra per diem, commissary privileges, and, more importantly, one hundred percent medical coverage. Yes, I knew I would be eligible to receive these "so-called" benefits, but they didn't take away from the fact that the pregnancy was unplanned and the child, unwanted.

Unlike my pregnancy with Charles years before, this pregnancy was a bit different. Jonathan and I were not even on speaking terms, and once again, I felt alone and abandoned. I plopped down on the chipped wooden chair in my sleeping quarters and allowed the tears to release. I was emotionally worn out, my mind bombarded with all sorts of conflicting thoughts—not being the most opportune time to have a child, not wanting to be a single mom, and the need to give the unborn child a chance.

Eventually, I dried my eyes, dressed for bed, and went to sleep with a firm decision having been made.

∞ ∞ ∞ ∞

I graduated from engineering training on July 17, 1995, right on schedule. I wasted no time leaving North Carolina and flew back to Miami to be with Charles and his family for my thirty-day leave before being transferred overseas. I made no mention of my pregnancy, and no one noticed.

On August 18, 1995, I boarded a plane in route to my first official duty station—Marine Corps Air Station Iwakuni, Japan. The flight to Japan was seventeen-hours, one of the longest flights I had ever taken. The sheer beauty of the countryside was mesmerizing. The temperature, though, was a sweltering ninety-nine degrees, and I was not prepared for the accommodating humidity. Like a kid in a wilderness camp, I was totally out of my element, culture-wise and food-wise. There was no Burger King or KFC. The only thing that resembled home were millions of little shops that mirrored New York City's infamous Canal Street, full of fanfare from one extreme to the other. The hot-ticket items during this time were silk sheets and mink blankets. Every Marine who lived in the barracks had a set because they made for a better night sleep in comparison to our regular itchy wool blankets and rigid 100-thread-count sheets.

I still hadn't disclosed my pregnancy to anyone and continued to work out vigorously as if nothing was wrong. I ate well, sleep well, and failed miserably at gaining weight. But after being in Japan for nearly two weeks, I became ill. I hadn't been this far gone in my previous pregnancy with Charles, so I was unsure whether the sickness was due solely to the pregnancy or if something else was going on. I went to Medical for evaluation, which only confirmed what I already knew.

With the official confirmation of pregnancy, I decided to set aside my pride and tell Jonathon I was pregnant.

I held my breath and pressed the last digit of his telephone number.

He answered on the second ring. "Hello," he said, with sheer unsuspicion in his voice.

The sound of his voice immediately brought me back to our beginnings. He was loving and passionate and went out of his way to make me feel special. I held the phone and did not readily respond until startled by the elevation in his voice.

"I said hello."

"Jonathan, it's me....Tiffany."

"Yeah, whatchu want?"

"I...I—,"

"Look, Tiffany, say what you gotta say....I ain't got all day," he said, cutting me off.

"I'm pregnant," I blurted out.

"And you want me to believe it's mine after you've been trampin' all over the base? Girl, you gotta be crazy."

"Jonathan, I didn't screw Wendell, and I didn't screw—"

He hung up in my face.

∞ ∞ ∞ ∞

The Marine Corp's Ball was held on November 11, that year. It was a yearly festivity when all Marines would put on their "Dress Blue" uniforms and come together in celebration of the Corps' birthday. Like many young unwed mothers, even though I was pregnant, I was immature. I was foolish and rebellious, refusing to wear my uniform because I just had to show off my new voluptuous body. To look at me you would have never known I was four and a half months pregnant. I was vain and far more concerned with being the "Belle of the Ball" than with the well-being of my unborn child. I wore a dress that was so damn tight it constricted my circulation.

By Thanksgiving, just a few weeks after the ball, I had cut off most of my friends and had gone into hibernation, and by the time Christmas had rolled around, I had fallen into major depression. Between the physiological effects associated with the pregnancy and the anxiety of being abandoned by Jonathan coupled with deliberate isolation from family and friends, I was emotionally depleted.

I made a second attempt to connect with Jonathon, thinking he might have had a change in heart since I was further along in the pregnancy and after possibly having realized that he was indeed going to be a father. I couldn't have been more wrong.

"Don't call me no more," he said, and hung up in my face once again.

I'll never call again, I vowed. I had to come to the painful conclusion that the whirlwind, sex-filled, fairytale of a relationship with Jonathan was dead, and I wanted to die, too. I went into my bathroom, pulled out a jar of aspirin, and shoved each and every one of them down my throat like they were candy.

I was found by my roommate some hours later, passed out on the bathroom floor. I was rushed to the clinic, where my stomach was pumped and my body infused with charcoal. During my hospital stay, which included being placed under suicide watch, I met with several counselors and therapists, and even a nutritionist, since I hadn't gained nearly enough weight for

 a woman who was going on five months pregnant. Follow-up intervention included outpatient therapy, in-home visits with a nutritionist, and subsequent prenatal visits with a perinatologist. But even after having pulled through the attempted suicide, I was left to do what we soldiers were taught to do—move on.

∞ ∞ ∞ ∞

In February 1996, I was transferred back to stateside in preparation to give birth. I was assigned to sunny California, Marine Corps Air Station, in El Toro, California. I lived out the remainder of the two months of my pregnancy preparing the baby's arrival. I was a long way from having the necessities needed for the baby,

 such as a crib, bassinette, car seat, etcetera, and those who were still associated with me where acutely aware. The following month, they (12 fellow male recruits) planned a surprise baby shower for me.

I was "showered" with so many gifts that I didn't have to worry about anything for the baby for quite some time.

∞ ∞ ∞ ∞

I went into labor on April 1, 1996, at approximately 3:00 am. As time progressed, the contractions were closer in proximity and became more intense. My faithful crew flocked in at different times, but nevertheless, came to support me during the labor. After some sixteen plus hours, my OB/GYN determined that I need to have a C-Section. So they prepped me for surgery and wheeled me in the operating room.

In less than an hour, I had given birth to a six-pound, four ounce baby girl. She had red curly hair, a pale complexion, and gray eyes. She didn't resemble me at all. But she was mine, and I fell intensively in love with her the moment I laid eyes on her. I named her Ariana, which means "Holy One." She was beautiful in every sense of the word. I couldn't wait to go home and lay Ariana in

the crib that had been cus-
tom made for her while I was
in Japan. I learned on this very
day that unconditional love
and the feeling of 'complete-
ness' was tied to becoming
a mother, even despite surrounding circumstances.

∞ ∞ ∞ ∞

My world began to fall completely apart on April 11, 1996, ten days after Ariana's birth. She had run a fever that I could not get to break, despite all the conventional and nonconventional methods I employed. She became increasingly pretty lethargic and slept a lot longer than she normally did. I was advised to bring her to the ER for evaluation. When we arrived, Ariana was snatched from my arms almost immediately, and the medical team went to work.

I learned that Jonathan had been deployed, so I put on my big girl panties and called his mother, even though she had previously made it known that she, too, had doubts about Ariana's paternity. Nevertheless, she must have put on her big girl panties, too, because she was cordial.

"I will see to it that Jonathan gets the message....And I'll be praying for her," she said.

"Thank you," I replied. I placed the receiver on its base, closed my eyes, and inhaled.

Ariana's condition slowly began to deteriorate after she had been in ICU for approximately five days. The doctors were unable to determine the cause of the fever nor keep it from spiking sporadically, as it had done over the course of her admission. She had developed a mild case of jaundice, which doctors passed off as "typical" for newborns. Being young and medically naïve, I took them at their word and didn't question further, initially. However, by that time, Ariana had been in the hospital three weeks, her food intake had decreased, and the size of her stomach became severely distended. The doctors presumed that her illness was associated with the liver and brought in a hematologist and hepatologist for specialist evaluation.

Iron Storage Disease. I had never heard of such disease, but that's what they determined was wrong with Ariana. As they explained it to me, with ISD, the body produces too much iron, which ultimately damages the liver and causes jaundice and a host of a lot of other things. When I learned that the cure for ISD was a liver transplant, my heart sank. I leaned over on Sampson, who was seated next to me in the ICU's conference room, and broke down.

"So what's the next step?" I asked the hepatologist, rubbing my sweating hands on the conference chair's hand rest after I had composed myself somewhat.

"We'll get her name on the donor and transplant list at Loma Linda Transplant center in Northern California."

I began to weep out loud again. This time, uncontrollably.

"It's gonna be all right, Tiffany," Sampson consoled. He was definitely like the big brother I wanted but never truly had—a guardian, protector, and close friend. But he was unable to comfort my bleeding heart in that moment.

On May 6, 1996, Ariana went into cardiac arrest. The medical team was able to restore her heartbeat, but she remained on a ventilator and in critical condition with her health fluctuating between minimal and modest improvement over the next twenty days. At some point during this critical twenty-day period, the doctors began to think that her ailment was caused by another condition and not ISD. My pregnancy history was probed, and before I knew it, my blood was being drawn for analysis.

Instead of the suspected culprit being ISD, it was now CMV, short for Cytomegalovirus Hepatitis transferred to her during my pregnancy. The doctors were vague in their explanation of the seriousness of the disease, which left me feeling a range of emotions, particularly guilt. *What had I given to my daughter?*

"How serious is this CMV?" I asked catching the hepatologist off guard when he had come back into Ariana's room to check on her before the end of his shift.

He hesitated.

"No B.S., doc. I just need to know. How serious is it?"

"It can be deadly," he said, dropping his head.

"Is my child gonna die?"

"Hey, let's focus on the here and now. We've sent your blood for analysis to a lab in Utah. Let's just see what the results are first. Then, we can concentrate on the baby's specific prognosis. This is a great hospital, and you have a team of great doctors on your side."

His words gave me some hope, and I actually felt better.

"You should go home and get some rest. The staff will take good care of your daughter," he encouraged.

I took him up on his suggestion and had Sampson pick me up from the hospital and bring me home. Of course I got no sleep. I kept waking up throughout the night thinking about Ariana. I couldn't wait until morning so I could go back to the hospital. I didn't have a car and didn't want to bother anyone with taking me back to the hospital in the wee hours of the morning.

∞ ∞ ∞ ∞

The lab in Utah confirmed my worst nightmare. I tested positive for CMV, which meant that I had passed the disease on to Ariana. It was evident that the disease had progressed to a very critical stage. The virus had severely affected her blood clotting factors and damaged her immune system. Recent tests, however, showed that her liver was beginning to show signs of regeneration, and that gave me some solace.

Jonathan had been notified of Ariana's hospitalization and grave condition via the Red Cross and was granted an emergency transfer from Italy to San Diego. Because of the tension between the two of us, and my whole unit, for that matter, Jonathan was escorted to El Toro by a high-ranking enlisted member of his command to meet with my Master Sergeant in an attempt to ensure that we maintained peaceful during the ordeal.

I gave Jonathan space to spend time with Ariana. I stood behind the invisible glass window and watched him—I didn't trust him. I watched him read to her twice and pick her up and hold her close to his heart. I saw a side of Jonathan that he had precluded me from seeing, his human side. I knew him to be a mean monster, void of emotion. But I saw something different this day. And I wondered....I just wondered.

On June 7, 1996, the doctors informed me that they had begun writing up a discharge plan for Ariana and asked me to admit myself into the hospital for three days so that I could be shown how to administer her medication, feed her, and receive training on how to properly care for her when she came home. So over the course of three days, I learned how to feed Ariana via a tube that was inserted in her nose and led directly to her stomach. She had lost the ability to suck and needed to be fed this way for the time being. Additionally, I learned how to administer the many medications that she required.

On June 13, 1996, Ariana was discharged from the hospital, and we returned home to our base housing. Jonathon came by a few days later, once again with an escort from his command to visit with Ariana. She was doing well, handling her medication as expected, taking her feedings, and becoming more alert and lively each passing day. His visit was short, for whatever reason. Our relationship was strained, and we were too stubborn and immature to fix it. Instead of allowing Ariana's grave condition to bring us closer, we allowed ourselves to be pushed farther apart. As cautioned from our higher ups, we were cordial, nonetheless.

"If you need anything, just page me," he said, handing me a piece of paper with his pager number and new address on it as he prepared to leave.

I'll admit, it was painful to see Jonathan walk out of the door that day as if he was just a concerned friend of mine and not Ariana's father. Beneath my anger and pain was a craving for comfort, and I wished he could stay.

∞ ∞ ∞ ∞

The morning of June 17, 1996, I got Ariana and myself dressed for church. I had planned a dedication ceremony at church for the both of us as a means of celebrating our new beginning. Throughout the day, however, I noticed changes in her behavior. She was sleepier than she had in the days prior, and she did not take her feedings as well as she had in the days prior either. I called Sampson, and once again, Ariana was rushed to the ER.

Ariana's condition was grim from the moment she arrived. Her liver had shut down and the vomiting was a result of the bile and formula that had backed up into her stomach. She was subsequently prepped for emergency surgery. I buried my head in Sampson's chest. He placed his arms around my limp body and helped me to the sofa in the waiting area. He was the sheerest embodiment of angelic presence. I let the tears flow, so much until the nearly the entire top portion of Sampson's T-shirt became soaking wet. It just didn't seem real.

"I need some aspirin, my head hurts so bad," I said, lifting my head, which by now, felt like one hundred pounds. I was dead smack in the middle of my life's worst nightmare.

"I'll go get some from the store," Sampson said, shifting his position on the sofa.

"No, that's okay. You don't have to leave," I said. Sampson's support was comforting to me during this time. I didn't want to be alone, not in this critical time. So Sampson stayed with me until he had to leave for work later on.

Per protocol, the hospital staff set me up to meet with a social worker. I met with her after Sampson had left. I fell asleep during our preliminary talk, having been exhausted from little to no sleep. I was constantly being updated on Ariana's medical condition throughout the day.

I don't think I had been gone from the social worker's office for an hour before I was notified that Ariana's body had gone into septic shock, and she was now in a coma. By the time I made it back to her bedside, I could barely recognize her. The patches from her surgery were bloody, and her hands and feet were blue due to the lack of circulation to her lower extremities. I could only stare at her in total disbelief, my heart bleeding on the inside. For a moment, I could no longer hear the background noise in my immediate surroundings. There was silence, a deep, penetrating silence. I closed my eyes and said a soft prayer. *God, if you hear me, please heal my baby.*

My prayer was interrupted by a gentle tap on the shoulder by the social worker that had come to lend me additional support. We had small talk about Ariana's condition, and she advised that the chaplain would be coming soon to pray with me, which he did, moments later.

"You really need to get some sleep," the social worker said, handing me a packet that contained literature on support services for families of critical care patients. "I've arranged for transportation to bring you home."

I nodded and took the packet from her hands.

"Someone will call you if your daughter's condition changes."

I walked out Ariana's room in a zombie-like trance, looking back intermittingly at her fragile body draped with tubes hanging everywhere. I felt completely hopeless, and my faith in the doctor's ability to save Ariana was beginning to severely diminish. So drained from the last two months of indescribable anxiety and fear, I headed toward the front lobby where the transportation vehicle was scheduled to pick me up, sluggishly dragging my feet along the way.

∞ ∞ ∞ ∞

I went home, crawled under Ariana's crib and fell asleep. I was awakened by the sound of the telephone ringing.

"Hello," I answered still half sleep.

It was a woman's voice on the other end. "This is Antoinette Preston calling from—"

"Is it my baby?" I screamed, cutting the woman off. "Oh, no, tell me she's not dead. Oh, God...tell me she's not dead!"

"Miss Duson, calm down...calm down. Your daughter is not deceased, but her condition doesn't look good. We think you should head on back down here."

I dropped the phone and went running next door to my neighbor's door.

When Sharon opened the door, fell into her apartment. "My baby!" I screamed.

"What's wrong?" Sharon screamed in equal terror, trying to lift me up.

"My baby....it's my baby. I need a ride to the hospital," I sobbed as I stood up.

"Let me get my keys," Sharon said. She went into the back room, grabbed her purse and keys, and we jumped in her car.

It seemed like it took forever to get to the hospital. But when Sharon did pull up, I jumped out and ran into the hospital. After taking the elevator up, I burst through the doors of the Neonatal Intensive Care unit and ran to Ariana's room, which was filled with doctors and nurses, and other medical staff.

I charged through her door but was confronted by a nurse who tried to keep me from going into the room. I pushed past the skinny nurse and opened the door. Dr. Adams was calling the time of Ariana's death as I walked in.

I fell to the floor and began to scream. "OHHHHHH-HHH, MY GOD...LORD, NOOOOOOOOO!"

The same nurse who tried to keep me from going into Ariana's room shook her head at Dr. Adams as if to acknowledge that she was unsuccessful at barring my entrance.

"It's okay, Dr. Adams," said to her. He stood over me as members of the medical staff helped me to my feet.

"I'm really sorry, mom. Ariana was my most challenging patient. We tried our best—we could not save her this time. She was just too weak...she's in a better place. She—"

I heard nothing else he said. The room went dark.

∞ ∞ ∞ ∞

When I returned home, I had an entourage of support waiting on me, including Cousin Antoine, whom I'd recently reconnected with, my friend China, my ace, Sampson, my girlfriend, Lucinda, friend, Jeffrey, and the base chaplain. They had been crying and mourning, too, evidenced their by red eyes and somber-plastered faces. I acknowledge them with hugs and went straight to Ariana's room. I walked around her crib, picked up her diapers and toys, and smelled her blankets. The thought of her never coming back was just too much to bear. I felt as though a part of me had died just hours prior, and the ache in my heart was too deep to massage and too new to even begin to heal.

∞ ∞ ∞ ∞

Everyone in my unit pitched in with helping to make the funeral arrangements. Master Sergeant Roberts saw to it that money was not an issue by soliciting donations from various agencies on the base to help cover the funeral expenses. I hadn't spoken to Jonathan, but I knew he had been contacted. He came by two days later with the sorriest of all excuses.

"I'm sorry. I lost my paper," he said, giving a weak apology.

"You lost something bigger than that!" I screamed.

∞ ∞ ∞ ∞

Ariana's funeral was held on June 24, 1996. Jonathon attended the funeral and sat by me for supposed support. I had already purposed in my heart that I would try to be amicable with Jonathan, as a final gift to Ariana. Since her conception, there had been conflict and tension between the two of us. So I vowed to let it go, even if just for this day. So I held on, trying to be strong, but there was really nothing left in me to fight. I felt weak and helpless, and when it came time for the procession to the gravesite, I collapsed in a sea of tears as I watched Sampson and three other comrades carry Ariana's casket from the hearse to the plot.

Ariana received a 21-gun salute, representing the full military honors. As the casket lowered, I lost it again, this time, having to be restrained. I came to myself at some point during the ride in the limousine. The remainder of the day was pretty much a blur.

Known Rehab

I never knew that danger could
hide in the form of family
That grief can be caused by the
loving embrace
Such truths tear away pieces of who I am
Shred the rope ladder to who I could be
And yet today I am free
Without reason other than that God can
override natural laws
And polish broken bones...and smooth
away brutal flaws
But I never knew such a world existed
Outside of the recycle "been" that I live in
Where Anita's been....and Mom's been
And I am forced to go
And learn things that a woman should
never know
And be taught tricks that a man should
never show
I think I am simply a fly...without any
fiery glow
Because I always end up neck deep
in crap
Perpetually lost in the valley of never-
will-be

Abandoned without the courtesy
of a map
Seams stretched so far...that the pattern
is now lost
Watching God weave new fabric...turning
old to new
A lifetime of rehab...heaven's currency
pays the cost
I wish I had never known...but yet and
still...I do

CHAPTER TWELVE

Reruns & Tantrums

In mid-December 1996, my request for a humanitarian transfer to Quantico, VA—the closet Marine Corp base to New York—was approved. The transfer permitted provided authorization for me to depart El Toro, California on February 1, 1997. I viewed my departure as an opportunity to leave behind the painful memories that kept me awake at night. The truth of the matter is, I never escaped the memories; I just buried them, and I would later learn that no matter how many times I relocated, my repressed feelings of hurt and anger would soon catch up with me.

I planned my road trip to Virginia in explicit detail. Chauncey, a close associate of mine, volunteered to utilize some of his leave time and accompany me across country. Together we packed up my newly purchased

Audi and hit the road on what would be a five-day, four night, seemingly, non-stop journey.

We arrived in Virginia on February 6, 1997, exhausted after having stopped in New Mexico, Alabama, and Atlanta for brief resting periods. The next day, I reported to my unit in full military garb, sharp as a tack. I met with the company commander, who assigned me to a dusty computer lab where I worked on broken down computers.

It was here that I met and bonded with a lady by the name of Lavonia Riddle.

Lavonia and I clicked, and immediately she took on a big sister role with me. She was a single mom, a Christian woman, and appeared to be well put-together and grounded. I confided in her early on about my loss, and she quickly became a listening post for me whenever I needed to talk and/or vent. She aided me in finally taking the photographs of Ariana off the wall so I could begin to heal. She was also instrumental in getting me to stop constantly watching the videos of Ariana's birth, suffering, and death. I sought refuge in our friendship, and her words of encouragement were therapeutic.

After multiple conversations on the subject of dating, Lavonia finally got me to agree to start dating. Through her, I met Miguel in May of 1997.

Miguel was of Brazilian and Guyanese descent. He was 5'5" and wore a tattoo of a lion above his heart. He was, by all accounts, a breath of fresh air, at least I believed him to be, in that season of my life. He was romantic and chivalrous, causing me to fall for him hard. Before I knew it, the dating process accelerated, and we prematurely walked down the aisle via the Justice of the Peace on August 10, 1997.

We moved out of the barracks into our own apartment the following weekend. Two weeks, later Miguel received orders for a one-year deployment to Okinawa, Japan. He was set to leave in roughly two months. He was new to the Corps, and it was mandatory that he serve a tour of duty overseas within his first four years.

A few weeks shy of Miguel's departure, however, I found out I was pregnant. Miguel and I were excited, as was his family and my friends. I spent half of my pregnancy worried if I would lose another child. Miguel left for Japan at the designated time, and I would carry out the remainder of my pregnancy alone, once again, and not just because of the physical separation. In all actuality, the story of my knight in shining armor ended before it began due to lies, deceit, and multiple episodes of infidelity on Miguel's part. We had rushed into the relationship, so I was a reluctant to work things through. I really didn't know the person I had married.

After he had been caught having one too many affairs, I went to the legal office and filed the necessary papers and sent them to him via FedEx overnight to Japan for signature.

"I'm not signing. You won't get half of what you want in these damn papers," he taunted, more concerned about losing material aspects than he was of losing his family.

"And I'm not taking you back, Miguel. You must've thought I was playing with you when I told you I wasn't going to be no dumb a** wife. I call you, and another woman answers the phone, and you think I'm gonna keep going through that? You got the wrong one," I said adamantly.

"We're gonna have a baby, and I want us to be a family," Miguel bargained.

"Then you should have thought about that before you decided to turn into Don Juan out there in Japan."

We went back and forth a few times before it was quite evident to Miguel that my mind was made up. I later learned that so was his.

Out of spite, Miguel had Toyota repossess the car we had purchased before his deployment, despite the fact that there were only three payments left. I was carless and couldn't get around like I wanted to. A few weeks later, a friend of Lavonia donated his beat-up car to me, and I traded it in for a Suzuki Sidekick. I didn't skip a beat. Miguel wasn't going to keep me down.

∞ ∞ ∞ ∞

On the morning of July 4, 1998, went into labor. I wobbled out to my car and drove some 40 miles by myself from Quantico, VA, to Bethesda Naval Medical Center in Maryland. I had been given the option of a having a repeat cesarean or attempting natural labor. I opted for the trial of natural labor. However, after enduring nearly eleven hours of excruciating pain, my

OB/GYN informed me that my cervix hadn't dilated more than one centimeter. With this news, I threw in the towel and opted to proceed with a C-section.

Indira, another beautiful baby girl, was born at 10:41 pm that same night. She weighed a little over seven pounds and was approximately nineteen inches long. We remained in the hospital for four days without any complications.

In the days I following, I was frantic, reliving the traumatic events surrounding Ariana's birth and subsequent death. Anytime a hair on Indira's head moved in the wrong direction, I would find myself rushing her to the hospital. Deep down I still blamed myself for Ariana's death, and I refused to take any chances this time around.

Although he had retaliated against me with having the car repossessed, I did the honorable thing and called Miguel and told him that I had given birth.

"What did you name her?" he asked.

"Indira," I said.

"You did?" he asked, shocked. We had discussed baby names shortly after I found out I was pregnant, and he fell in love with the name Indira. So he was shocked that I still named her Indira, especially after what he had both said and done.

"Yes, I named her Indira," I confirmed.

Neither of us said anything for a few moments, and the silence made me uncomfortable. The divorce was still pending, and I didn't want to discuss it, but obviously, Miguel did.

"Are you sure you want to go ahead with the divorce?"

"I'm sure," I said. I was in automatic mode by this time, having made so many mistakes when it came to relationships. I didn't want to be alone, but greater than the fear of being alone was the desire not to continue to be a battered and abused wife. I was more focused on being the best mother I could possibly be for Indira.

By the end of September, my divorce was finalized. I was a free woman who was also extremely impulsive. Repeating the pattern, I didn't stay single for long, I went right into a new relationship without adequate emotional recovery.

∞ ∞ ∞ ∞

Indira was all of six weeks when I met Langston Townes. He, too, was a Marine who was stationed at Henderson Hall in Arlington, Virginia. I was captivated by his good looks, his charm, and his provider mentality. He was brown skinned, stood about six feet, six inches and was muscular. I thought he was perfect for both me and Indira, and he stepped right in and immediately took on the role of a father figure in Indira's life. He did everything from changing her diapers, rocking her to sleep, feeding her in the middle of the night, and playing with her daily. Early in the relationship, I knew I was dealing with Miguel's twin, in the sense that he was a lying, two-timer. But I had gone fast speed ahead with him from the very beginning, and there was no turning back. The romance was steamy, the sex, addicting, and the co-dependence, convincingly clear.

Of all the men I had dated or married up until this time, Langston would have the greatest effect on me. I had a thousand reasons to walk away but always ended up being swayed by Langston's sweet talk, sympathetic apologies, or his impulsive and violent temper. I wasn't afraid of him, my low self-esteem made me believe I needed him for one ill-fated reason or another. In addition, the culture of the military promoted very traditional values—pursuit of the military career and achievement, marriage, being a parent, and subsequent retirement—and I knew I was failing miserably at the attainment of all of these things.

Although Langston thought he had his bases covered, he was sloppy, and I ended up driving to the home of one of the women I believed he was messing around with, just to confront him.

Initially, there were no cars parked in the driveway, and I wasn't bold enough to ring the doorbell, so I waited outside in my parked vehicle to see if Langston would show up. I waited there for nearly four hours before I spotted a blue Toyota Corolla pull into the driveway. Langston's truck followed right behind the Corolla.

Intuitively, I knew something wasn't right. My heart began to pound. It was show time, and I hadn't exactly planned how I was going to confront Langston. He had a bad temper and wouldn't hesitate to put his hands on me.

I started my engine, put the gear in reverse, and pulled in the driveway behind the Corolla. I spotted that the person inside the car was a woman, and that's when the adrenaline rush kicked in. I jumped out of my car, ran up to her car, and swung the driver side door open.

"Did you know he had a girlfriend?!" I screamed.

"No...I didn't," the woman answered, taken aback.

By this time, Langston had gotten out of his car and was walking around his truck over to the two of us.

"She's crazy. Don't listen to her, Evelyn," he yelled to the woman, simultaneously grabbing my arm to pull me away.

"Look, Langston, you and her work whatever out. I told you I don't do this kinda drama," the woman said, getting out of her car and slamming the car door behind her. She strutted into her house and left us outside in a screaming match.

"Why the f**k are you here?" he said, successfully using his brawly strength to pull me to my own car.

"Get off me!" I shouted. "You lying, cheating bastard! Get the hell off me!"

"And you get the hell outta here, you home-wrecking bitch!" He was angry, probably angrier than I had ever seen him before.

After a few moments of staring into my eyes, he finally let go of my arm. I waited until he had walked up the driveway and up the front steps to the house before I ran to the back of my truck and grabbed a Tropicana bottle that I had filled with coins. I held it over my head and threw it at Langston's truck.

He flew back down the steps and came charging at me. I lay down on the ground and put my feet in the air, causing Langston to go flying over my head. He landed on the pavement and rolled. I knew he was coming for me, so I jumped up, ran to my car and locked the door. Feeling defeated, he jumped into his car, started the engine, and sped off. I cranked my engine once again, put the gear in reverse, and followed him. I was seething with anger and unable to get ahold of my emotions, not enough to stop and let it all go. I already had proof he was cheating, and his total disregard and lack of respect was clearly evident, so why did I feel the need to chase him through town and nearly run him over? Low self-esteem, undoubtedly.

When it was all said and done, Langston and I exchanged a few other words and drove off in our separate ways.

∞ ∞ ∞ ∞

I had not had communication since the night I confronted him at Evelyn's house. I was trying to move ahead, but truthfully, I was painfully lonely and wanted missed him. Surprising, however, he called me just a few weeks after the incident and apologized. I played the role, though.

"I hear you apologizing and all, but you've got to do something about that cheating," I demanded, as if it was truly a deal breaker.

"I just want to start over, no going back over the past. Let's start fresh. It'll be different, it'll be better," Langston promised.

Against my better judgment, I bought into the falsehood and the vicious cycle would soon repeat itself.

After we were both honorably discharged in 1999, he, in January, and I, in April, Indira and I moved in with Langston, partly out of desire and mostly out of necessity—we had nowhere else to really go. So Langston and I played house for the next year plus, going through the motions but never making any real plans to move the relationship further. The truth of the matter was that we were both psychologically addicted to pain, rejection, and abuse. Our twisted relationship was more about the void and fear in our lives than it was about anything else.

I joined Harvest Life Changers International in Woodbridge, Virginia, after having been invited to attend by my friend Lavonia. Physically, I wasn't separated from Langston, but emotionally, the process had begun.

By June of 1999, I wanted a change of scenery and a much-needed break from Langston; he had become extremely possessive and was emotionally raping me daily. So, I decided to take Indira and go somewhere far away from him. I called Aretha, a mutual friend of ours and asked her if I could come stay with her in Atlanta to sort of check the area out. Without hesitation, she opened her home to me and Indira.

"Yeah, girl. Come on down and check it out. Is Langston coming, too?"

I paused. While she knew Langston and I had our share of troubles in the relationship, she didn't know to what extent, and she certainly didn't know that I was trying to leave him.

"I take it he's not," she guessed.

"Rea, I just need to get away. I'm tired...I'm just really tired. I need something different. I'm—." I couldn't finish my sentence. I just let it out.

"Girl, it's going to be all right," Aretha consoled. "You and that beautiful baby just come on down here. You don't have to worry about anything, just come."

"Okay," I said, softly sobbing.

So one day while Langston was at work, I packed up my truck with Indira, hit the road, and drove the eight hours to Atlanta.

I wasted no time getting out and learning my way around the City. I lined up a series of interviews. But after being frustrated by the lack of employment offers, Aretha and I decided to take a night out on the town at the local pool hall to relax. It was here that I met a man named Darryl. Darryl was a "bad boy" in the truest sense, a well-known drug dealer in Atlanta. But nonetheless, it didn't scare me, and I let him wine and dine me. I didn't have financial issues when I was with Darryl, but the limbo status of my relationship with Langston brought drama, including the threat of Langston killing me. I knew I was putting not just myself, but other innocent people's lives in danger. I broke it off with Darryl.

By late August that same year, I packed up in my vehicle and headed back to Virginia to so call "work it out" with Langston. Fearing my safety, Aretha begged me not to go. But I, still psychologically addicted, went back for "more."

∞ ∞ ∞ ∞

The abuse started back up almost immediately. Instead of being greeted with the open arms he claimed to have had, I was berated with slurs and accusations.

"So who you been f**king down there in the great big A.T.L, huh?" he said, tugging at my pants.

"Langston, please. You're gonna wake Indira up," I pleaded.

He pushed me down on his bedroom floor and stood straddled over me. "I don't date hoes, and I know you've been in Atlanta hoeing 'round town."

As much as I wanted to, I knew not to try to defend myself. The truth of the matter was that I had ended the relationship with Langston before I left for Atlanta. So technically, I could have slept with anyone I so chose. But I was desperate in that moment and needed place to stay. So I kept my mouth shut.

"And you have nothing to say?" he instigated. My silence had irritated him. Before I could utter a word, he grabbed me up by my neck and threw a hard punch right in my left jaw. My head jilted back. The force of his punch gave me an instant headache. He released his grip and I fell backward, almost hitting my head on the footboard post.

He kneeled next to me and begin to rip my clothes off.

"Langston, please," I begged. I was not in any mood to have sex with him, and I was too weak and exhausted to fight him off.

"Shut the f**k up," he said, ripping my underwear off. "We gon' see if you been sluttin' around," he continued, shoving his right index and middle finger into my vagina.

I screamed out in pain. "Please, Langston, please stop! I ain't been with no one," I lied. There was no way he could tell if I had or hadn't had sex. What he was doing to me was a terrorizing and humiliating act.

"And you gon' give me some, too. This is mine, bitch...mine," he said, unbuttoning his pants.

I lay like a zombie as he brutally raped me, alternating between forcing his penis and his fingers in my vagina. I didn't scream audibly, but on the inside, my soul was screaming—murder!

When he was finished, he rolled over on the floor and passed out into a deep sleep, at which time, I jumped up, grabbed one of his long T-shirts that was lying on the dresser, and went to check on Indira, who, miraculously, had remained asleep during the entire ordeal. I lifted her up over my shoulder and crept into the darkened entryway of the kitchen. I flicked the light switch on and scanned the counter to see if the cordless phone was on its base. I tiptoed over to the phone, picked up the receiver, and dialed 9-1-1, cupping my left hand over the earpiece to drown out the sound of the dial tones.

"9-1-1. What's your emergency?" a male voice answered.

"My boyfriend just beat me up," I whispered. Protocol followed, and I provided the 911 operator with my name and Langston's address. I locked Indira and myself in the hallway closet and waited for the police to arrive.

The sound of the doorbell must have awakened Langston, because I could hear him shuffling around the in room. I burst through the closet door, ran down the hallway, and opened the front door, holding Indira over my shoulder.

"Someone call the police at this residence?" the police said after I had opened the door.

"Yes," I said, out of breath. "I called. My boyfriend beat me up," I said, bursting into tears. By this time, I could hear Langston's footsteps behind me.

"Can we come in?" the heavyset, white male officer asked. There were three officers, two males, one black, one white, and one white female.

"Sure," I said, opening the door wider and reaching over to turn on the light switch in the living room. By this time, Langston had made his way from the bedroom to the living room where he was met by the staring eyes of the police officers. He was fully dressed and didn't look disheveled in the least bit. As a matter of fact, he appeared as calm as a toad in the sun. I, on the other hand, looked as though I had run from Freddy Krueger.

"Sir, did you physically assault your girlfriend?" the black officer asked, retrieving his black report book from his back pocket.

After observing my face, the female officer diverted her attention away from my face to my torn clothes. She raised her eyebrows and turned to radio in a code of some sort.

"Officer, we just had a simple disagreement. She hit me,

and in self-defense, I pushed her off me. I mean, she could have fallen against something," he lied, trying to explain away the bruising on my face and swelling of my jaw.

"We're going to need to talk to you guys separately," the female officer said, reaching for Indira who was beginning to wake up. "I'm going to put her down on the sofa, okay?" she said, sorting of asking but more so telling me.

"Sir, do you mind going into another room?" the black officer said, walking up on Langston. He seemed to have little patience and didn't believe the lies that Langston was spewing.

"Not at all," Langston said, leading him toward the kitchen. He was a good actor, and I hoped that they could see through his antics.

The female officer waited for a moment and then asked, "Do you feel safe in here, or do you want to go outside to talk to me?"

I turned to see if Langston was looking, but he had disappeared into the kitchen with the two male officers. I nodded. "I can talk in here. I don't want to leave my daughter," I said.

"Well, first let me introduce myself. My name is Officer Charlotte Spivey. You want to tell me what happened tonight?" she asked, retrieving her report book from her back pocket as well.

I provided details on Langston and my tumultuous history up to and including the events that occurred earlier. She took meticulous notes and asked if I wanted to press charges.

"Do I have to?"

"No, you don't have to, but you might need to. Guys like your boyfriend in there won't stop. Sometimes, the abuse ends in death."

My mind immediately went back to Langston's earlier threat to kill me, and he almost had, on more than one occasion.

"You don't have to do anything you don't want to do," she continued. But he's going to jail tonight just based on the fact that we see evidence of an assault, which we're going to need to take pictures of. If you decide not to press charges, that's on you. But like I said, he's going to jail tonight no matter what. You can stay here tonight knowing that you're safe, at least for the night. If you think you need to go to the hospital, I just radioed for the paramedics, and they're on their way."

"I don't want to go to the hospital," I said. I didn't want to leave Indira behind with anyone. And I certainly didn't want to give Miguel any ammunition to accuse me of putting her in an unsafe environment.

"Do you have anything else you want to say to me?" she asked.

"No," I said. I had the feeling that she knew I had been raped but wasn't going to pressure me about it. I purposely did not report the sexual assault because of fear of retaliation. And there was also a part of me that didn't want to ruin his professional reputation. I figured that a few nights in a cell for the physical assault would cool him off and teach him a lesson.

"Here's my card. If you have something else to add, call the number on the card. Someone from the D.A.'s office will be in touch with you."

I took her card. We sat on the sofa until the paramedics arrived, asking and answering questions intermittently. Officer Spivey escorted me outside when the paramedics radioed in. She took a slew of pictures of my face, arms, back, and legs. I was treated in the back of the ambulance, given antibiotic ointment and an ice pack. As I was being escorted back into the house, the two male officers were escorting a handcuffed Langston out of the house. He tried to make eye contact, but I turned my head in the opposite direction.

∞ ∞ ∞ ∞

Weeks later, Langston's forgiveness plea came in the form of a proposal to build me a home, and I fell for the trap. I had gone through hell with him, and the proposal appeared to be an adequate tradeoff.

We moved into a townhome until the house was finished. Shortly thereafter, I found out I was pregnant. The

OB/GYN's date of conception traced back to the night of the sexual assault, and I realized that I had followed so many patterns that my mother had, no matter how much I claimed I didn't want to be like her. It was frightening. But I found solace in the belief that if I stuck it out long enough, went through the abuse, and waited it out, it would all pan out for the good.

In the following weeks, I tried to live as normal of a life as I could by assimilating myself into the corporate world. Although Langston and I were still having relationship woes, we were still "technically" an item, and my dream home was still in the process of being built. I guess you can say that I settled for Langston, because deep down I knew he could give me no more than what he had already offered. I was pregnant, however, and this time, I was determined to fit into society's bracket of normalcy by having my child live in the house with both parents, no matter what the cost.

I was fooling myself, however, if I thought I was experiencing any ounce of normalcy. Nothing had truly changed. Langston still had affairs. As a matter of fact, during the pregnancy, he had a lively affair with his boss, and blatantly refused to end it. He continued to lash out at me verbally and physically, enough so that I went into preterm labor, three times!

On April 18, 2000, at only thirty-three and a half weeks, our son, L.J., short for Langston, Jr., of course, was born. He weighed 5 lbs. and 11 ounces. L.J. was

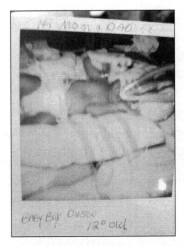

a big boy and would have doubled his weight had I gone full term. He was rushed to the Neonatal Intensive Care unit, hooked up to breathing machines, and given intravenous fluids. Looking at him in critical condition gave me a flashback to Ariana. By now, I had tried not to think about her too often. In some ways, I felt that Indira was Ariana, just in a different body.

Nevertheless, L.J. remained hospitalized for a little more than five weeks to allow time for his lungs to completely mature, and he was sent home in late May, a few days shy of my birthday.

∞ ∞ ∞ ∞

On June 1, 2000, we moved into our newly-built home. Technically, we were a family, but we were so far removed from one another emotionally. By now, I was fully aware that he and I were basically going through the motions, even though we had entertained the thoughts of getting married. Truth be told, I was more consumed with decorating our new home than planning a wedding I knew wouldn't last.

Our townhouse was beautiful, nevertheless. It was a three-bedroom home, with fifteen-foot ceilings, plush white carpet, and a two-car garage. The master bedroom was designed with a master bathroom equipped with a Jacuzzi tub, single shower, and dual sinks. We had his and her walk-in closets, and of course, I selected the larger of the two. The kitchen was customized to my exact specifications, since cooking was my forte, and I knew I'd be in it quite often. It was designed with hardwood floors, green marble countertops, black-on-black appliances, cherry wood cabinets, and a fabulous breakfast island in the center. We turned the basement into a family room, and sectioned off the unfinished bathroom for upgrade at a later time. We had a modest front and back yard. Taken together—the house, the children, and the nice cars we drove—we appeared to be the picture-perfect family that we were far from being. If it wasn't for the fact that we slept in the same bed, Langston and I would have fit the definition of roommates, because we certainly didn't share interest in extracurricular activities, particularly attending church services. He didn't attend, and he didn't want me to attend either. This, too, sparked disagreement and strife in our relationship.

∞ ∞ ∞ ∞

I suffered some financial and emotional setbacks when I got the courage to leave Langston. I went from job to job and eventually became homeless, living in boarding houses until I could stabilize my income. Langston took advantage of my misfortune and filed an emergency petition for custody of L.J. Although we were awarded joint custody, L.J.'s primary residence would be with Langston. This bitter dispute set precedence of our relationship for the next two years.

In 2001, Langston sold our home and moved to Maryland, making it a little difficult for me to have daily visits with L.J. One particular afternoon, however, I went to pick L.J. up from daycare, and Langston and I got into it.

"I wanna talk," Langston said, in his usual condescending tone.

"I don't have time," I said, cracking a fake smile for L.J. who was looking at the both of us.

"What do you have to go running off to? It ain't like you clocking dollars at some job and gotta rush back," he criticized. It was a deliberate insult, which he had always done. But for some reason, this time, his insult felt like a blow in my chest. He was taking unnecessary jabs at me for being between jobs.

"I came so I can spend time with my son, and I don't have time for your BS," I said, rolling my eyes. I didn't want to give the slightest indication that I was offended by his comment.

"Well, if you ain't got time to talk, you won't be spending time with our son," he said, trying to grab L.J.

That's when I snatched L.J. up, jumped in my car, and sped off. In turn, Langston jumped in his car and chased me. I sped down Highway 95, and he followed. At some point, I must've lost him, because I could no longer see him in my rear view mirror. Feeling defeated, Langston ended his pursuit and called the police, reporting that I had kidnapped L.J.

The police showed up at my door and demanded I return L.J. to Langston or be taken into custody for kidnapping. It nearly killed me to have to return L.J. to Langston, but I realized, in that moment, that if I was going to make a home for my children, I needed to take responsibility for me, make some dramatic decisions, get myself together, and be the best mother I knew how to be.

I called L.J. from the bathroom where I had him hid and relinquished custody once again to Langston.

CHAPTER THIRTEEN

Double Daddy Issues

After several rounds of interviews and lots of strategic planning in my personal life, I landed a great job working as an Executive Assistant for a private charter plane design firm, took pride in rearing my daughter, and used some measure of caution in building new relationships. After the separation from Langston, I found myself at square one, searching for the acceptance of others, in particular, a "man" without the negative by products of rape, degradation, deception, and abuse. I even entertained the idea of consummating a relationship with a woman, an idea that isn't really foreign to women who have been abused and become scorned as a result.

In July of 2001, I transferred positions within the company and joined the Federal Aviation Administration's Security Equipment Integrated Product

Team (SEIPT) where I worked as a Materials Specialist and Project Assistant. I was responsible for going into Airports delivering presentations, selling, and obtaining Airport buy-in for the Security Equipment that scans luggage at airports. My career was taking off, I had become even more visible than before on the professional front, and as a result, more career driven and less concerned with having a man on my arm.

Soon enough, I was being invited into private venues, art galleries, embassy functions, and celebrity homes where men of all ethnicities and statuses flocked. It wasn't long before I laid on my charm so thick that men began throwing money at me. I was, however, dishing it out, making demands and being accepted for who I was pretending to be. In my mind, I'd given up on love, and I was sick and tired of people taking me for granted. It was time I took charge.

With the money came the VIP invitations, Ritz Carlton's Suites stays, Watergate bashes, shopping sprees, jewelry, limos, a personal assistant, Manolos, Gucci, St. John, etcetera. What I didn't anticipate was the exchange of "favors" and "arrangements" that came along with the territory. I could hear Momma Mason's words playing as a recorder in my mind, "Nobody gets something for nothing." But I was too caught up in the emotional high ushered in by fast money, and lots of it, and the vast attainment of material things.

The summer came and went quickly, but not before I had caught the eye of a gentleman whose name shall remain anonymous. To protect his identity, I'll call him *David*. He was an astute businessman and CEO of a highly-regarded private security firm in Maryland. He stood 5'4", was a little on the chunky side, and was not at all soft on the eyes. I wasn't concerned with his looks, though, because what his physical semblance lacked, his bank account made up for it.

In the early stages of our relationship, I got everything from David that I demanded. He was very attracted to me, a younger black woman. I was more like a bratty child that thought I deserved everything and wanted my "daddy" to pay for it. Our "secret" relationship provided me with an allowance of $5,000 a month plus living expenses. In exchange, I accompanied David to dinners at extravagant restaurants, galas and other events, and provided him with sex on demand. Outside of these parameters, I was free to live my life as though he didn't exist. I spent a great deal of time shopping and working. I hired help for my daughter, traveled extensively, and stayed in five-star hotels everywhere. But suddenly my lavish lifestyle was put on pause.

The events of September 11, 2001, had direct effect on my company, causing my position to be eliminated. Thus, just weeks before Christmas, I was laid off. The next few months for me would prove challenging. I had grown weary of looking for a new job every so many months, and I wanted out of DC, longing for yet another change of scenery. Since the attacks of 9/11, I had managed to isolate myself just about everyone in my circle. I didn't have a lot of money, so I knew I would need some financial assistance from none other than the Mister... David. All I simply had to do was ask.

After having wild, kinky sex with him, I sat up and struck up the conversation. "You know, I was thinking."

"You're always thinking," David said, exhausted from the escapade.

"No, seriously. I was thinking that I've been looking for a new job every six months or so, and it's getting very tiring. It's taking a toll on me."

"So?" he said, sitting up.

"I want to go to a place where the economy is good and jobs are not so hard to come by. I want something permanent, to be honest. I'm tired of temp jobs."

"So what area are we talking?" he said, moving my hair out of my face.

"New York City."

"New York City, huh?" he said as if he was trying to imagine me there.

"Yeah, I'm sure I can land a job there in no time."

"And if you don't?" he said, smiling.

"I....I'm gonna need you to stick around then," I said in candor.

"You not taking your daughter with you, are you?"

"Nah, I think I'm going to let her stay with her god-parents until I get up on my feet."

"Yeah, you might want to do that," he encouraged.

"Are you willing to at least help me get there?"

"Where are you going to live?"

"That's a non-issue. I have tons of friends...friends who have already said I can stay with them as long as I need."

"You still need a plan," David cautioned. After all, he didn't rise to his position in the corporate world without being financially savvy.

"I have one. I don't plan on staying with my friends for long. I've already started applying for jobs. You know me, I can get a job quickly."

David paused, not sure of cosigning on my proposed timeframe but then followed with, "What do you need?"

"A couple of thousand," I said, knowing he had it to give.

"And when do you need it?"

"Yesterday," I joked.

David gave me the two thousand dollars, and just like that, the plan was in motion. I had both a will and a way. Motivated by the same impulsivity that had me running from myself for nearly thirty years, I moved to New York City within a few weeks. My plan, however, required a bit of modification—the warm invitations into the home of my friends were rescinded. I was left living out of my Saturn.

In late January of 2002, I landed a temporary job as the second Administrative Assistant to Ronald Blaylock the founder, chairman and chief executive of the institutional brokerage and asset management firm, Blaylock & Company, Inc., located in Downtown Manhattan. When I felt comfortable enough, I used the office as a temporary residence. My daily stint would begin between 5:00 and 6:00 pm. I'd leave the office pretending that I was headed home. When the office cleared out, I would sneak back into the office with my key. I would almost immediately close the shades. I watched TV in the conference room until I got ready for bed later on in the night. My nightly routine included brushing my teeth and boiling hot water in Ron's coffee pot to take a bird bath. I'd munch on leftovers in the refrigerator, if I didn't have a few bucks to go next door to buy myself a small meal. At the end of the evening, I'd then curl up on the sofa in Ron's office and go to sleep. My alarm was set for 5:00 am, at which time, I'd awaken, get dressed for work, leave the office, and go to the bodega next door to buy a bagel and cup of tea. By the time I finished my breakfast, I'd stagger back into the office with the other employees as if I was coming in from "home" as well. I kept this stint going until I finally mustered up the nerves to tell David I was homeless. He sent me more money, and I secured an apartment in Jersey City.

My temp assignment with Ron lasted for a few months before I was offered a permanent position. I was later let go because I lied on my application, and my past had caught up with me. I had written some bad checks when I was homeless while living in Virginia. With no one else to turn to, I called David once again, who this time, gave me luring proposition. And I accepted. I signed up to be a kept woman.

∞ ∞ ∞ ∞

Once I got up on my feet, I began traveling extensively between New York and D.C. I had plenty of money to take care of my household expenses, get my hair done weekly, have my hands and feet manicured as needed, and even send money to the kids. Who needed a job? I traveled all the time, networked and attend events all over the City, and even became known for throwing lavish parties and serving expensive food and wines, everything from Beluga Caviar to Crystal Champagne.

David and my "arrangement" would soon go from excitement to boredom, for David. He wanted me to engage in explicit public acts and the ultimate act of sharing my bed with another woman. To him, I was being paid for a service; therefore, his requests weren't unreasonable. I didn't want to give up my meal ticket, so I agreed to honor his requests. Besides, I knew Indira's birthday was around the corner, and I wanted to give her a big bash, you know, the typical guilt party. Since I wasn't there, I felt I had to make it up to her by throwing her an extravagant party, not fully realizing that all she ever truly wanted was my "presence" and not presents.

I took David's American Express Platinum card and splurged on gifts for Indira as well as purses, shoes, and clothes for myself. I had to give the appearance that all was well. But even after the shopping splurge was over, I still couldn't handle full parental responsibility for Indira, Langston still had primary custody of L.J., and I was still in dire need of a stable job with sufficient income. But thinking about it, made my head hurt—it seemed out of reach.

I knew how to alleviate these feelings of despair with clubbing, drinking, or lying in the arms of a man. Although they carried negative long-term effects, the short-term pacification was satisfying.

∞ ∞ ∞ ∞

I met Alexia through a mutual friend. Alexia was in Atlanta visiting her best friend. She was a tall attractive woman, with smooth dark skin, and long flowing hair. I could tell immediately that there was something between us, but I dared not try to articulate it. After being introduced to each other and engaging in preliminary chit chat, we exchanged telephone numbers and planned to link up for dinner and paint the town red during her stay.

And partying, we did! On our way back to our hotel one night, Alexia broke out a pack of purple (marijuana). I had never done drugs of any kind, but my senses were heightened from the alcohol in my system, so I took a few puffs. And when I woke up hours later, I was lying naked across the hotel bed. I didn't remember how I had gotten out of the limousine and in my hotel room. The entire room was pitch black. I sat up and scooted over to the edge of the bed, my head pounding. I tried to remember the earlier events of the night but couldn't. I had lost recollection of the entire past few hours. As I turned my head to the right, Alexia and her friend were lying naked, side-by-side. My stomach began to churn, and I leaned back on the headboard and dozed off, partly because of the effects of the alcohol and marijuana but mostly because I didn't want to face myself and the act that I had just engaged in.

I was awakened by Alexia's hands rubbing on my lower back and sliding down my buttocks while she was simultaneously kissing her friend. I froze, but I closed my eyes and let it happen. After all, I had been contemplating being with a woman and felt that I could use the sexual encounter as a barometer to determine whether becoming a bisexual or lesbian altogether was for me or not.

When the sexual escapade was over, I ran to the shower and turned the water up to borderline scolding. It seemed as though the moment my body touched the water, I became convicted in my spirit. I had committed an abominable sin, as they used to say. I reached for the soap bar, lathered by washcloth, and tried to scrub every ounce of guilt, disgust, shame, and disgrace off me. Grandma Anita had taught me well.

When I returned to my apartment in Jersey City days later, I began to reflect on my life. I had spent the past six months being homeless (living out of my Saturn on the freezing cold streets of Manhattan), surviving the freezing cold temperatures by sleeping in the office bathroom of one of this country's top investment bankers, Ronald Blaylock, to living in a brownstone in Jersey City, NJ that was being paid for by a pimp, basically. By my standards, however, I felt I was doing better than most. But my soul wanted to be free. I knew what it took to pull myself up by my own bootstraps, and I was even more ready than before, even though only weeks prior, I was content with being a kept woman. It wasn't my destiny, however. I knew I wanted better and could do better. But I'm a living witness that the road between knowing better and doing better can certainly be a long one filled with roadblocks and detours.

∞ ∞ ∞ ∞

By the end of July 2002, I had landed a job as a private contractor with INNOLOG, a Virginia based logistics firm. They hired me to join a team of special project managers who would assist Homeland Security with the transition of at least four hundred Airports from private to federal oversight. The pay was great, but it required

ninety percent travel. I decided to take the job anyway—
my spiritual independence depended on it.

Indira stayed with her godparents a great deal of
the time while I was on this assignment. I had been
making more than $65.00 an hour and lived out of my
suitcase in more than twenty-five states the ninety-
day project period. But as most contractors know, the
projects would eventually end. So my goal shifted from
simply looking for "work" to looking for a permanent
job at other companies in the Aviation Security sector of
transportation.

Before the end of the assignment, however, destiny
had called my name. The buzz had traveled fast about
a young, twenty-five-year-old fireball—"Tiffany Duson,"
of Virginia, and her New York dream team. Our business
success garnered the attention of CEOs from top For-
tune Global 500 businesses, and my business genius and
astute problem-solving acumen soon garnered me the
prestigious position of Terminal Operations Manager for
San Francisco International Airport.

Here I was, twenty-five years old presented with
an opportunity that was far beyond my qualification
and one that an African American simply did not occupy in the aviation industry and especially at my young
age. I knew the position would bring about much strife
because there were some politics that preceded my
arrival, which I was prepared to conquer. A man by the
name of Carlos Mosby, who was a mentor to me, had

briefed me well in advance. Nonetheless, I jumped at the opportunity that allowed me to bring my two core leaders with me. And within weeks, I closed out the Oakland Project, resigned from INNOLOG, and moved to South San Francisco. I hired a nanny, moved Indira back to live with me, and enrolled her into Montessori School. We were building our lives again.

My new role at SFO came with much excitement, challenge, stress, but also long, exhausting hours. I worked most days from 4:00 am to 8:00 pm, sometimes seven days a week. I thought that if I could keep myself busy, I'd lose my sinful cravings and kill any time I had to recreate my past lifestyle. But a busy routine as a substitution for what my flesh had developed a ravenous appetite for only lasted four months. David, ironically, didn't stay too far removed either, as he continued to wire money to my account on a monthly basis. The spider web cycle was still in full effect.

∞ ∞ ∞ ∞

It didn't take long for the tension to start at the new job, which included hate and racist emails, name calling, and work sabotage. To combat the assaults, I fought with every weapon in my arsenal from the EEOC to the NAACP. I filed complaints with every organization I could identify. While I was firing back, the company began illegally fighting back against me. My fight for fair employment practices of team ended badly. I heard the dreaded phrase once again.

"Tiffany, I'm sorry, but we're going to have to let you go."

"You're letting me go?" I said, flashing back over the significant impacts and achievements I had garnered while there.

"I'm afraid so."

"Why?" I challenged.

"We like your work, but we just don't feel that your team is a good fit for the company," they lied.

I knew it was more than the "good fit" reason behind the firing, and I wasn't willing to lie down without a fight. I pursued legal recourse, and we settled out of court for wrongful termination in the later months.

No sooner than my legal battle with Covenant Aviation Security ended, did another ensue—I received a summons to relinquish my place of residence. My world was caving in once again. This time, the set-back landed me in a psychiatric hospital where I was diagnosed as manic depressed, a diagnosis I staunchly denied.

"I don't care what you say, I'm not crazy," I said to the psychotherapist, who was a black woman who looked to be just a few years older than me.

"I'm going to be brutally honest with you, Mrs. Duson. The longer you stay in denial, the longer the staff is going to think you have a problem. If you want out of here, you should consider cooperating on all levels. And that means talking with me, taking your meds, being nice to staff members, as well as other patients. It's simple as that," she said, before getting up to grab another writing pad.

I suppose she was right and was only trying to help me. And I did want out of the psychiatric hospital because I didn't think I was crazy or on the brink of catastrophe. So I decided to take her advice and play the game.

I stayed hospitalized for several days and was released with several medications that were supposed to "make me better." Truth is, no pill had the power to reverse my psychological and spiritual ills. I had lost confidence in myself because I had been knocked down several times after I had worked hard to pull myself up. So I did what I was accustomed to doing—search for rescue.

I registered on the dating site, Match.com, and met Roland Reynolds, CEO of a software development firm. He was a great conversationalist who could speak and converse on any topic. He had the gift of gab and would tell you whatever you wanted to hear. My initial impression of Roland Reynolds was that he was the Brooks Brothers poster boy. But boy was I wrong! He was a square during the day but a nympho at night. His sex drive was exceptionally high, and he didn't want just sex; he wanted excitement and thrills, which drove me to revert back to my faux bisexual tendencies. I began discreetly soliciting women online via various websites frequented by couples, because I wanted to please him. And I honestly believed that I could meet his needs and have a healthy open relationship that wouldn't force me to compromise...at least not too much. Wrong, again!

By November of 2003, I lost my home and Roland and I moved in together. My move became one of survival, and I found myself forced to compromise with Roland's antics just to keep a roof over my head. I tried to find a way out of the open relationship that I basically signed up from day one.

"Babe, maybe we can just work on us," I said one night, trying to convince him that a monogamous relationship was what "we" both needed.

He chuckled. "If it ain't broke, ain't no need in trying to fix it. I like us just the way we are."

Fearing being on the streets or in a shelter, I acquiesced, never bring the conversation up again. I knew I had to develop an exit strategy, because the relationship with Roland wasn't going anywhere.

∞ ∞ ∞ ∞

One Sunday in March 2004, after a night out on the town clubbing, dancing, and drinking myself into stupor, I woke up behind the Greyhound Bus Station on the corner of San Pablo and 20th Street in downtown Oakland. Coincidently, there was a church directly in front of where my car was parked. I didn't recall how I had gotten there. Voices of passersby's, who were dressed in their finest attire, awakened me from my sleep. I watched them as they cut across the parking lot and made their way to the church, ascend the church steps, and disappear behind the glass-stained doors. Something in my soul stirred, something I couldn't articulate either. So I promised myself that I would attend services there the following week. Maybe church was where my greatest strength and abundant blessings lie.

The following Sunday, I courageously walked through the doors of Greater Saint Paul Baptist Church. Earlier in the week, I had gone to my storage lot and pulled out my best suit, wrinkled and all, and had it dry cleaned. I went to the salon and had my hair styled just right. Lastly, I put on my mask, trying to hide behind my sinful nature from the previous nights, days, and weeks.

We Wear the Mask –
by Paul Dunbar

WE wear the mask that grins and lies,
It hides our cheeks and shades our eyes,
—

This debt we pay to human guile;
With torn and bleeding hearts we smile,
And mouth with myriad subtleties.

Why should the world be over-wise,
In counting all our tears and sighs?
Nay, let them only see us, while
We wear the mask.

We smile, but, O great Christ, our cries
To thee from tortured souls arise.
We sing, but oh the clay is vile
Beneath our feet, and long the mile;
But let the world dream otherwise,
We wear the mask!

It was my first time going to a church in more than two years, and it wasn't one that I had previously attended. But I knew the protocol, the flow of service and how things were supposed to go—smile when embraced and bless others when blessed.

I stood in the lobby and was greeted by a member of the Hospitality Committee.

"Is this your first time here?" an older grey-haired woman asked.

"No," I lied. I didn't feel like going through all of the formalities with writing my information on cards and speaking with Brother and Sister So-And-So afterward.

"Well, do you already have your seat?" the usher, sporting her black skirt and white blouse, asked.

I shook my head, and she led the way, escorting me to a pew on the right side of the sanctuary. I sat through service, clapping my hands to the joyful sounds of music and nodding my head to the on point snippets of the pastor's sermon. Bishop Sampson, the pastor of the church, announced the invitation to salvation, I sprinted down that aisle to the altar, sobbing profusely and begging God for restoration and restoration.

I "officially" accepted Jesus into my life in April 2004. What happened over the next year would set me on the course to liberating and life changing experiences! I tried God, despite what it looked like. I would now learn how to navigate my way through.

CHAPTER FOURTEEN

Still Navigating...

By March of 2004, I had saved up enough money to gain permanent shelter, having gone to the Internet café and search Craigslist for room rentals. I caught a break and found a room to rent two blocks from the church I attended, utilizing my unemployment and food stamps to barter with potential landlords. Simultaneously, my health had become somewhat challenged. I suffered from recurring acute bronchitis and underwent two emergency surgeries for ruptured ovaries, so my recovery impeded the process of me finding employment and getting up on my feet.

I finally secured a new job at a dot.com company in their account receivables department, earning $42,000 a year, which was a significant pay cut. But things appeared to be looking up. Pretty soon I worked my way to having my own place to live. Although I was doing better and living what I deemed a purer life, I wouldn't, however, escape the repercussion of the sins of my past. I had to answer to charges of theft and fraud, stemming from writing bad checks, albeit done for my survival, and welfare fraud from collecting public assistance monies while working. I lost the job at the dot.com company for lying on my application. I was still in a very painful place in my life, but it was exactly where God wanted me.

A year would pass, and I was gradually healing and slowly rebuilding! I found another temp job and had worked and earned enough money to afford a studio apartment on 10th Avenue in Oakland, found a roommate, and upgraded to a two bedroom, and then eventually to a three-bedroom apartment, all within a year. Finally, in February 2005, I was beginning to experience some measure of peace in my life.

By now, my daughter had returned home and I had built up a local support network. I had a roommate and together we began raising our children and splitting our expenses. I became more active in my church and joined several ministries from the choir to praise dance ministries. During this time, I finally mustard up the courage to start my own company, "The Impact Group, LLC," and built new relationships that later lead to new clientele that generated new business and networking opportunities. With much persistence, I garnered needed certifications and began to gain some much-needed exposure to grow my business. By August of 2005, I secured my first business development contract in Morocco and would begin my first assignment on a ten-day tour in Northern Africa with a US Delegation that I pulled together with the help of my Arabic and French interpreters. My company was the lead Project Management Team. We assisted two US FIRMS develop the necessary strategic partnerships needed to obtain access to pursue multi-million dollar maritime security contracts with the three major ports in North Africa.

God had given me extreme favor, allowing me, as a woman of color, to leverage my former Federal Aviation Administration relationships and enabling me to obtain meetings with the Moroccan Government. I was a Lead Project Manager conducting business in an Arab Nation where women were not allowed to speak openly, let alone sit at the table with men. This was nothing short of God's favor!

Little did I know another storm was brewing, one, however, that I was better prepared to navigate my way through. *This* time.

CHAPTER FIFTEEN

Seasons must Change

I was ready for a new season! It was time for a change of scenery. AGAIN! I had outgrown Oakland and was ready to start afresh somewhere else. I remembered a contact that I had met back almost a year prior just by happenstance while I was visiting Utah, and I reached out to him. His name was Earnest Davis, a prominent businessman, Marketing Executive and Voice-Over talent based in Atlanta, Georgia.

"I'm looking for new consulting opportunities, and I was thinking about relocating to Atlanta," I said, seriously contemplating a more permanent move.

"As a matter of fact, I think you're calling at the right time. Do you think you can be here in forty-eight hours? I want you to meet my team." he said.

It was a few days shy of the 4th and I jumped at the opportunity. My friend Christine offered to let Indira stay with her for the brief time that I would be there. I landed that afternoon at 8:00 pm. Earnest picked me up at the airport, we talked briefly, and I crashed hard in his guest room. When I woke the next morning, it was all business; he had scheduled a meeting with two of his business partners and myself. Earnest and his partners owned natural hair care salons around Atlanta and were working on some other side projects. Earnest identified an opportunity that would help leverage his company's skills in marketing and business development and wanted me to assist them in their salon expansion endeavors.

During the meeting, I would meet Robin Groover and David Farnum who were also partners at the Too Groovy Salon & Spa. And at some point, Robin leaned over and said, "You're coming to Atlanta for me, and you don't even know it yet!"

She and I connected instantly. Robin was a Natural Hair Care expert, and at the time, was working for Design Essentials while she built her own empire. After our meeting, I returned to Oakland the next day and immediately put together a proposal to begin negotiations. I needed some time to think about what I would need to make a transition to Atlanta work! I was excited that things were easily coming together for me. *The time is right!* I thought.

Upon my arrival home, however, I was greeted with FBI and Oakland Police Department business cards stuck in my door. One of my nosy neighbors, a white woman named Vicky, approached as I walked to my apartment door.

"The FBI's been around here asking a lot of questions about you. They've been showing pictures of your daughter asking if we've seen her," she said, with a look on her face as if she was expecting me to admit to some type of crime.

My heart raced as I skimmed the cards over.

"And they've come around here more than once. Better watch out, before someone squeals on you."

"Thank you," I said to Vicky, simultaneously unlocking my front door.

"You're welcome," she said.

I lifted my suitcase, opened the door, and went in my apartment. I immediately called the number to reach the Oakland detective who advised that I was wanted for questioning related to a kidnapping.

"Kidnapping my own child?" I said, almost laughing.

"We're merely enforcing court orders established during your divorce," the detective said.

"What orders?" I said, obviously oblivious to what the detective was referring to, and he sensed it.

"Ma'am, I'd get a hold of your divorce decree as well as the enforcement order, if I were you."

"I will," I mumbled, trying to remember what terms I was bound by that would render me a kidnapper of my own daughter.

It took a little investigation, but I finally got to the bottom of the ordeal. Using unscrupulous tactics, my ex-husband, Miguel, was able to obtain a sole custody order of Indira and came to California to take her from me. He had resurfaced and was seeking to cause havoc in my life once again. I plopped down on my bed face forward and began to cry. I was tired of fighting, and yet I found myself in another battle. I was exhausted from the years of getting up, falling down, getting back up, and falling back down. The cycle was draining, but nevertheless, I still had some fight in me. I wasn't going to just lie down and let him win.

I immediately hired and retained the services of my family law attorney, Linnea Willis. After obtaining all relevant court documents she called me into the office for a meeting.

"How have you been?" she asked, sorting through a pile of paperwork on her desk.

"Not sure," I said, taking a seat. I wasn't sure just how I felt at the time. I had been through a lot and had become very guarded, and even paranoid in some instances.

"Well, I have good news and bad news. Which do you want first?

"The bad," I said, taking a deep breath.

"I've been able to determine just how your ex-husband was able to pull this tactic off. First of all, he's well within his right, under the laws of the Uniform Child Custody Jurisdiction and Enforcement Act (UCCJEA) to file a report against you for kidnapping. The law is tricky, sometimes. But your divorce decree briefly outlines that parameters of you guys' joint custody agreement."

"So what's the good news?" I said, anticipating some lame action I would have to take to "meet Miguel halfway. "

"We can beat this thing. You won't have to give primary custodial rights, but you have to be willing to fight both hard and dirty."

"Dirty, like what?"

"Find something...anything on him. He's going after you with everything he's got, so you have to do the same."

I grit my teeth. Her words penetrated my being. I was no punching bag, and I made up in my mind to fight, although I would have never imagined that a man I once loved and conceived a child with would come after me with such vengeance as Miguel did. He and his attorney attacked my character to the core, accusing me of being addicted to crack cocaine, using my brief stints of homelessness to render me as unfit, and also using my employment status to claim I didn't have the financial means to take care of Indira. But I fought hard, and I knew God was on my side.

While simultaneously navigating the raging waters of this legal battle, I opted to pack up my Oakland apartment and take on the consulting project with Earnest and his salon partners in Atlanta. When my contract was finalized, we came to terms that his company would cover my relocation expenses, provide me with a $5,000 down payment for a new car, cover my housing expenses and provide me with a $1500 stipend. The deal was set in motion, and I moved to Atlanta, Georgia on Labor Day weekend in 2006, with nothing but three suit cases and the clothes on my back. I couldn't legally or permanently leave California, because it would have impacted my child custody case—I left many things behind, including Indira, who was in hiding. This time around, I was determined to win at LIFE!

∞ ∞ ∞ ∞

Christmas Eve came, and so did my children! I had my daughter flown into town and L.J.'s father dropped him off at a mutually-agreed location. It was the first time I had seen my L.J. since the previous summer, without an argument with Langston, Sr. I promised myself that I wasn't going to concentrate on the negative, only the positive. And I did. I was just happy to have my children under one roof.

My son stayed with us for two days before I had to relinquish custody of him back to his father, and Indira stayed with me for one week before I flew her back to California to keep her in hiding.

The consulting gig with Ernest didn't pan out to have the longevity we initially expected that it would. I had some monies saved, but traveling back and forth to California for the custody hearings took a great chunk of it, and my savings were running out. I became homeless once again resorted to living out of my car. In my arsenal was the fact that I had navigated these waters plenty of times, and I knew it was only a matter of time before my persistence and perseverance would pay off.

In the meantime, however, I had to wear the mask and was forced to pretend like all was well. I didn't announce my troubles, I continued to attend church, be an active participant in the various auxiliaries, and search for more work. I received small monetary gifts from churches and one church member who claimed God had laid it on her heart to give me two hundred dollars. I graciously accepted the money and used it to pay for a room at a boarding house down in the Bankhead district of Atlanta. Two hundred dollars would cover my shelter for at least a week, so I was content. I was taking it a day at a time. Anything beyond that was subject to grace.

When I ran out of money, I took shelter in apartment garage on Penn Street, just south of Ponce De Leon in Atlanta. During the day, I hung out at Starbucks, bakeries, and coffee shops, living out of my trunk and bundling up in massive amounts of blankets. But sometime in late February 2007, I finally broke down and confided in a friend and told her my true situation. I was referred to a member of our church who gave me immediate refuge in a spare room in her home. The climb up this mountain would be slow one, but I had no choice but to climb.

The custody battle with Miguel became even nastier, as he and his attorney were hit with the legal blows that my attorney had thrown at them. God was truly on my side in this battle. In the end, full custody of Indira was granted to me, and Miguel was ordered to pay $756.00 per month in child support. *Case dismissed!*

Now that the tumultuous court battle was over, I could finally bring my daughter out of hiding. I caught a glimpse of the light at the end of the tunnel. I wasn't at the end, but the glimpse was sufficient enough.

Life went on, the holidays came and went and by February 2008, I was out of another job at FedEx Smartpost. After peak season, the staffing firm that hired me to manage their operations onsite was forced to scale back their staffing budget, which meant layoffs for their Executive staff. My head was on the chopping block.

By now, however, I knew that there was something else going on—God had not called me to a job but to ministry. So I was able to chalk up my history of job losses, lay-offs and terminations as God pulling me to my destiny. The unfortunate thing was that when these things were happening to me, I couldn't see past the immediate incident. There was a very obvious pattern occurring in my life, because every time I got comfortable and reached a certain level of successes, God removed the job and closed the door.

∞ ∞ ∞ ∞

With some measure of financial success, I was able to purchase a home in Georgia. L.J. came to visit me and Indira and enjoyed himself so much that he asked to stay. Surprisingly, Langston allowed L.J. to come live with me.

Senior Human Resource Officer for a MARTA contractor called MATC.

My new position bought me much professional success, thousands upon thousands of dollars into my household, and in nearly two years, I was honored as the top 40 under 40 in Human Resources throughout mass transportation. *I wasn't doing so bad,* I thought. I had gone from living in my car, to a boarding house, to a room, an apartment, another apartment, to now to owning my own home. I also had both my children under one roof, and I felt as though my life was coming together.

One day in January of 2009, Langston showed up without notice, having taken offense to the way I disciplined L.J. This particular day, he showed up in the middle of the afternoon and trailed behind L.J.'s school bus. When the bus driver let L.J. off at the designated bus stop, Langston snatched him up and took him back to Maryland. And just like that, my happy home was abruptly disrupted.

Son, wherever you are, make no bones about it.
I love you and will always love you. I've never stopped,
and you are deeply missed!

After the incidence with Langston taking off with L.J., one storm after another kept popping up. On the eve of the Super Bowl in 2009, I received a call from my friend Antwan, asking for a ride to the hospital to be with his sick girlfriend. I agreed to take him, jumped in my car, and headed over to his house to pick him up. As I passed Hartsfield-Jackson International Airport exceeding the speed limit, I was pulled over by the College Park Police. As I waited for the citation, I observed another police car pulling up to the scene. Two officers emerged from that car and they all three walked to the driver side of my car

"We're going to need you to step outside of your vehicle, ma'am," the young, white male officer who originally pulled me over said.

"What's going on?" I asked.

"You have a fugitive warrant in Florence, South Carolina for embezzlement," another officer answered.

After spending twenty-one depressing days in the Fulton County jail, I was extradited to South Carolina, where I successfully hired counsel to represent me. We went before the magistrate judge, who, after hearing the charges, released me, citing erroneous charges that were not criminal. She also found that the company who filed the initial complaint had abused their power.

After my release, I was placed on a greyhound bus and shipped back to Atlanta, which turned out to be less than eighteen hours of my arrival. I later received a letter of apology and dismissal from the Florence County Courts! *Yes, I sued them!*

But my troubles didn't end there. I had another run-in with the authorities on April 25, 2009. While speeding to get to Indira's AAU basketball game, I was pulled over by the Powder Springs Police. When the officer ran my license, it came back as suspended, even though I had the documentation to prove otherwise.

"I'm going to be all right," I said, trying to console Indira, who immediately sensed a repeat of the previous arrest.

"Look, don't talk to her. You're getting arrested, and she'll be placed with the Division of Child Protective Services. Now, step out of the car before I snatch your ass out!" he yelled.

"Don't tell me not to talk to my daughter!" I yelled back, handing my daughter my cell phone. Call 9-1-1 and tell them we need a supervisor."

This must've made him angrier, because as soon as I stepped out of the car, the officer snatched my arm.

"Get the hell off me," I said, trying to pull my arm away.

"Give me your hands!" he said, using what I deemed to be excessive force.

I was able to free my hands, and when I did, I ball up my right fist and punched him square in the middle of his chest. He lunged for my neck and ended up grabbing my left arm and swinging me down to the ground. We scuffled around on the ground, he pulling my braids, and I, biting his arms. The other officers intervened and pulled me and the officer off one another.

When all was said and done, I ended up being arrested and detained by immigration because the authorities were suspicious of my identity. I was also charged with obstruction, a charge that is considered a felony.

 After putting my house up to satisfy a $10,000 bond, I was released. After hiring counsel once again, I went back to court, and the charge for driving with a suspended license was dismissed due to an error on behalf of the Driver's Bureau. However, the felony stuck, and I ended up receiving court-supervised probation under the first offender program in Georgia, and later having the record expunged.

∞ ∞ ∞ ∞

Money spent on my legal affairs left me nearly penniless. My cars were subsequently repossessed, and my home placed on courthouse steps for foreclosure. I filed bankruptcy twice to fight the foreclosure process but then rescinded the filings, giving up the battle with the banks.

CHAPTER SIXTEEN

A Turning Point

M y daughter and I had lost everything and I had hit rock bottom, again. Little did I know that God had already opened a door that would forever reshape the course of my destiny, one that no man could close!

Shortly after the announcement of my impending layoff in 2010, a stranger on Facebook in-boxed me and offered me an opportunity to own my own travel home-based business. Initially, I snubbed my nose at it, until I realized that I needed money and companies were *not* hiring

(Donald Bradley, Mentor & Coach)

me. The light bulb came on; the way to freedom was helping others become free.

CHAPTER SEVENTEEN

She Speaks (The Epilogue)

The healing process has been unconventional for me, however in each storm, my life has come together, in purpose and meaning. I lie in bed one night listening to a CD of my former Pastor, Bishop Sampson preaching on the subject of "Elevating Your Expectations." I realized that my "Moses", "Job " and "Joseph" experiences" were all apart of "God's Vision," and that He was simply ready for me to elevate my expectations of him and for my life.

I learned the art of speaking to things as if they already existed, and I have come to expect nothing less than success from my adversity. After all, I am on a path of perseverance and restoration!

My life, by far, is not without fault, and I can truly and safely say that God is still working on me. Since I've begun sharing my story publicly, I've entertained a multitude of questions and comments, some to the tune of "How are you still sane", "Can you prove it", and, of course, the doubters who simply say, "All these things couldn't have possibly happened to one woman." There are two questions, though, amongst the believers that stick with me: "Have you healed?" and "Have you forgiven?" My response is two–fold, yet it pours out of me fluidly: *But God!*

I have a clear understanding of why I made certain choices in life. But I have also embraced the teachers, because I have learned so many valuable lessons. Secondary to this, in my life, forgiveness has become a mandate. Next to both of these, I adopted a love for myself that is hard-matched. I've gone from extreme turbulence after takeoff to a pretty smooth landing.

How has all of this unfolded? I learned what it means to truly walk by faith and took a chance on Him. Truthfully, many chains had bound me in the past, causing me to fall on my knees and seek God for deliverance countless times. I have searched the scriptures and claimed many verses, only to find the chains were still attached at various points. The seeking, without finding lasting deliverance, brought about much frustration, anger, and at times challenged my faith in God. Many times, I felt hopeless and alienated, as if God really didn't care about me.

My past has always tried to control my present and give me a black eye and a bleak-looking future. Many of my wounds were indeed self-inflicted as a result of generational curses, which I've begun to break. I've adopted the mindset that my pain is result of the enemy's attempt at my demise and destruction. Satan somehow gained head-way in the lives of my many abusers. For where I should have found love and support, I received torture, abuse, criticism, judgment, condemnation, hurt, and loss of identity. When I finally looked back on my life one day while sitting in Roland's loft, I began to ask God for revelation, psychoanalyzing the failed relationships, the pains and hurts, the trials, tribulations and situations.

My transparency has become my weapon of choice. It is what I use to disarm the enemy. When you put everything is out there, nothing can be used against you, unless you allow it. It can only teach you. I took on the word of God as my instruction manual. I told God to allow me to deal with each hurtful area of my life as it was. I reminisced on His promises and the vision He had given me in my "Moses and Job experience." As I began to think about each plague and painful memory, I could feel His warmth and His love flowing toward me.

His eyes were fixed on me. He was healing me from the pain of my past.

From that point on, I could no longer see the painful moment—it was as if my memory had been erased. And as I focused on God, I could no longer hear the bantering of my grandmother, or feel the rape of the strangers who violated me at a tender age in my youth or that of Langston, the beatings of the past, the men cheating on me, or harbor on the failed relationships, the bisexual episodes, and the adulterous affairs. I could no longer feel the pain from the rejection of others. And even though I believed that I had forgiven my grandmother in 1994 while she was on her deathbed, God required me to do it again.

Today, I am still tested, and I still experience various forms of rejection and adversity on other scales. The difference, however, is that I am not moved by them, and it no longer matters what happened yesterday. I don't live there anymore, and I've learned to navigate my way through. I can overcome ANYTHING through Him.

Learning to see God in everything, everywhere, and in everyone has brought a great measure of comfort, peace, joy, and normalcy to my life. I stopped praying for God to help me. Now, I simply ask Him to "Do it." And I expect that he will. I've elevated my expectations. This statement, although simple, is profound and has changed the way I pray and live. In the past, I didn't think to walk by faith; I operated on my own accord. After all, I believed for so long that I had to lean and depend on myself, and I thought "man" could save me. When I reflect on the past, I fell short and lived in guilt. In many instances, I blamed myself profusely. The guilt later turned to frustration and anger. I hated who I was, and in turn, I lashed out at the one person who had the power to right every wrong—God! I blocked out and abused anyone who tried to come close to me. I thank God for deliverance and for His way of living, because I no longer need to be bound by certain rules and regulations that society says I should follow; I take pleasure in "defying the odds"—I no longer need to please man or flesh. I reverence in my gift to "Speak" to any mountain and it be moved.

I want to deposit this sentiment into your life! I love you! My reverent prayer is for you to resist urges of self-destruction because there is a way out, and someone is listening. Allow no one to silence you! SPEAK UP! SPEAK OUT! SPEAK LIFE! Your past does not determine your future. You are stronger and bigger than your situation. I don't care what it looks like. I know deep pain, but I now know forgiveness and healing. I know that it could only have been God that brought me thus far; it is His love that has kept me focused on breaking the generational curses and cyclic behavior that once kept me bound. I am focused now on my personal ministry of bringing others "out." The greatest victory is to never lose sight of what God promises you! Your haters, naysayers, and enemies have no power to block them. They might try to, but they do not have the power to block what God has released.

If you're a victim, like me, you must now become the victor, which comes with knowing that obstacles are merely the things you see when you allow your fleshy focus to dominate, which opens your spirit up to the attacks of the enemies, memories of the past, depression, fear, anxiety, worry, self-pity, improper thoughts and attitudes, guilt, accusation, inferiority, hopelessness, sadness, anger, deep hurts, sickness, religiosity, an impure heart, anything that is negative and anti-God.

This is a message to everyone who is at his or her wits end:

Who can say you won't be back when they don't even know where you've been? There's strength in your bones, way down in the fires of your soul. Stretch your hands towards Heaven, and your forces will unfold. This is a wakeup call—Come out of your trenches. Mother, tell your daughter, and fathers, tell your son! You've got to tell your testimony, because it wasn't designed for you. You've got to get your personal message out. You've been silent for too

*long. Death and Life rest in the tongue.
Mother, tell it; Daughter, know it. Father,
speak it; Don, declare it. The breaking of
day has finally come your way. When you
open your mouth, you can have whatever
you say. Speak to the wind, the rain, and
the trials and tribulations. God has saved
the best, and it's coming right to you.*

If you've not done so already, pray in your own way, as best as you know how—because much prayer equals much power, and I've done a great deal of it and now have much power.

You've must see your victory and what you want, live it as though it has already come to pass, because what you see in life is what you get.

My expected results in life don't leave me a lot of time to be miserable or to keep a lot of people in my life. I've learned to depend on God's grace to get me through the day and on the power of prayer to elevate me to the next level. I found the part of me that rested deep within, that part of me that had nothing to do with any other person or anything external. I've been blessed to discover that it's only about me and who I truly am. The part of me that has nothing to do with any role I played, or the expectations that others have of me. I found the part of me that has always been there, watching, observing, and recording every moment of my life.

That part of me is now unleashed and excited about this new journey. I've been reborn in the spiritual and physical realm.

Thank you for allowing me to come into your heart and share my story with you. Every odd and adverse situation you face can be defied.

~Chinaza

Embrace the Journey...

I n the words of Maya Angelou:

I am a human being—therefore nothing human can be viewed as alien to me. It is not our thoughts that create our reality. Would you not agree? You see, I've learned that when one's energy and vibrational frequency is in alignment with what is to come one's way, there is nothing that can truly be denied to you.

Like Maya, I, too believe that there is a space created that has allowed the unification of my fleshly being with my spiritual purpose to pulsate to the rhythm of my once hill street blues. And for what it's worth, perhaps the beauty in this all perplexes a piece of even me. I'm in a space where I grateful for the opportunity that I have been given to walk through a welcoming, embracing corridor, and while I don't always get it, I know now that God does. He has given me beauty for the ashes. I have moved into a space where I can earnestly thank Him for the opportunity. Yet there are still moments when I feel I can't, or feel as though it's too hard. But I possess the unmitigated courage to touch, love, live, and thrive no matter the problem *(I refuse to admit that I'm frighten beyond my wits)*. God has become my refuge; I've just never been one to call it quits. You see, I dare to just be ME. I dare to be bigger than any condition, circumstance, or situation. I dare to stretch myself.

Daily, I sing and pray, sing and I pray, I cry and pray, a good cry, cleansing of my soul, my frustration, and then I begin to bless the space that I'm in. Yes, I will be okay, my life does go on, and I have made a concerted decision to not be bitter, no matter how the tide turns or wind blows. In the end, no one knows. We simply must embrace the journey.

This new season in my life represents a fundamental turning point. The inception of new dreams, new guidance, renewed purpose, and new relationships have served as a form or validity that the universe has enabled me to see. I am too anointed to remain anonymous. God dreamt a dream bigger than I did for my life, a dream I could never dream for myself, and there is no age limit placed on the dream.

Finally, I have learned to live in the space of letting go! What will the universe have me do next? I'm not sure. However, I know there are no longer limits. Yes,

I've got more character than a Shakespeare play, but the difference between me and that which stands in between, is that I am brave enough to take a look at my wings and take flight.

Now how I've come to be—it has been a journey indeed! Again, I reference Maya Angelou when I say, *I've have had so many rainbows in my many clouds...I am now prepared to be that rainbow in the clouds of others!*

(Mommy & Daughter, January 2015)

USDA Choice

It is unavoidable
But that doesn't mean that you wont try
to avoid it...deter it...and evade it
That would be like hoping the sun doesn't
come up tomorrow
And yet at Marie...the light comes
And so does the suffering of destiny
The weight of what lies before you...
grappling with who you are today
Imagine a seesaw...with you on one end,
and a huge weight on the other
The weight on the other end is Promise.
Who you could be, and what you
could achieve
That's enough weight to easily lift you
high...but there's a problem
Most of us are not free to be lifted
Most of us carry too much weight...
for our lives to be sifted
The pressures of life, the ripples from
bad choices...
Drama of our own creation, the sediment
of listening too long, and hearing
wrong voices
These are weights that lay upon your
heart and shoulders

And flood the recesses of your mind
So the seesaw doesn't lift you...instead
it brings pressure
Because destiny is trying to lift you...
and life is struggling to keep you down
And therein lies the Suffering
Like when you try and watch a video...
and the computer says that its buffering
It's preparing the footage...the subject...
so that it can be viewed
Your future is trying to do the same...
but it has one obstacle...YOU
So as I said in the beginning...
it CANNOT be avoided
But the path that you take is 100%
your decision
You can carry unnecessary weight and
get squeezed in the process
Or you can stay free...and let the coming
future, lift you above that mess
Be of a sober mind...and absorb the
message of this book
The author has revealed her story...
and was brave enough to share her voice
Not a person on this planet can
hide from it
The Unavoidable Suffering of Destiny...
but always a Choice

Acknowledgements!

(Chinaza Duson with son and daughter - Photo Above)

First, giving honor to whom much honor is due, for without God, Jehovah Shalom, this book, this season, this moment would not be possible. I give you all the praise, honor, and Glory.

To my Grandmother: May you rest in peace.

To my Granddad, my forever guardian angel, may you rest in peace! You told me when I was a little girl that I would change the world, and I will. Thank you for preparing me for such a time as this. I love you!

To my Cousin "Antoine": You know who you are, and I love you. Always know that cream rises to the top!

To Momma & Poppa and Lil Sis: Thank you for taking notice of me that day at Gateway Children's Home and for bringing me to your home!

To my biological mother: I'm letting it go. For you did the best you could, given the circumstances, and I thank you for not aborting me! My life, as you know, has never been the same, and I'm glad about it!

To my brother Russell: Thank you for taking care of Mom and for being my brother.

To my mentor, my big business dad, and his beautiful bride—Donald & Deborah Bradley: Thank you for pushing me to a holistic, wealthier place!

(Chinaza Duson, Donald Bradley, Tonya Mizelle & Melodie Washington)

(Julanda George, Chinaza Duson, and Tim George)

To my sister from another mister, Julanda George, my ride or die chick, my shoulder to cry on, my confidant, and my brother, your Sweet Tea, Tim George: Thank you for allowing me into your family and for running right long beside me. Chloe and Gavin, Auntie Chi loves you!

To Jackie Pippins: We've been through hell and back, through thick and thin, our eyes have roll and crossed, but yet they've locked on a common ground, and our hearts have stayed true to the cause of being in service of others. Thank you for money, food, a car to drive, an ear to bend, and a partnership that will last for a lifetime. I still want to get our DNA checked. I love you. Thank you for welcoming me into your home. You truly are the biggest and the baddest, and I'm grateful to God you're on my team in business and in life!

(Chinaza Duson & Jackie Pippins)

To Clayton Sizemore, my Yogi: Oh my! What a journey we've had. You've taught me how to breathe and just do me. You have been the wind beneath my wings and a close confidant. I will forever love you. Thank you for allowing me to serve as your fearless leader!

(Chinaza Duson, Clayton Sizemore, T-Rhone, Pastor & Brydzetta Knotts, Momma Watkins, Jason Cross, JP Watkins & Tonya Mizelle)

To Naomi: The UK isn't ready for us, but we leave them no choice! Let's get it done, my sister!

To J. Cross—Mr. President: Salute to you general. I am eternally grateful for our friendship and partnership!

To Nichole Bess-Hawkins: We could go years and not speak (like now)! I still love you, and I know that no matter how many times we don't see eye-to-eye, you're still my sister!

To Bishop Lester Love, thank you for mentoring me in ministry, for showing what it meant to have excellence, and more importantly, for allowing me to serve as the sole ghostwriter on your "Art of Amor Bearing" masterpiece. You taught me that as a gatekeeper in the Kingdom, one must first serve the dreams of another before God will bring your dream to past.

To Tonya Mizelle: Thank you for becoming the total confidant for the night in Dubai. As I prepared to leave, you said, "We are sisters". And we are. We just don't share the same blood. I want to also thank you for introducing me to Reggie Joe (so that smart girls can retire rich), after Raimon Norris nagged me relentlessly to get it together.

(Chinaza Duson & Tonya Mizelle)

To Reggie Joe: Thank you for being my financial planner and for helping me stacks these coins!

To Lionel and Cheryl Woodyard: Thank you for standing in the gap and being my parents by proxy! I love you. You make me proud to call you mom and paw-paw!

To Dr. A: I put all my business out there now! Thank you for your friendship!

To Roniel Sylvester: "Started from the bottom no we're here!"

To Shedrick White, my partner, and The League: We are the dream team ordained by God in this season to break poverty and reshape the destinies of many! I rebelled at first, but I'm so glad to be partnered with you, and I'm also glad were going straight to the top!

To Radika Bailey: Thank you!

To Nicole McDaniel: Thank you for your love, your prayers, and for the birth of "She" on ice.

To my entire FIRM FAMILY: Without you there is NO me!

To the entire Paycation Family: You simply rock!

(Raimon Norris & Chinaza Duson)

To Raimon Norris: You came into my life on a painful rebound, and although our agenda wasn't in the cards, you've patiently stuck around, allowing us to get back to the purpose of why God brought us together. You've held down the home front, you've served me and my family relentlessly, and you've put up with all my craziness in this pursuit of purpose. You have created the visual branding and given presence through your company Rehobath Media to Chinazaspeaks a.k.a. Shespeaks for pennies, and it's been priceless to the world. You've been the man, the silent observer, the instructor, and now you continue to serve as my greatest asset, a secret weapon, and my amazing personal assistant and media production manager. Regardless of which way the wind has blown this butterfly, you're right there with the net! I'm grateful. I've learned many lessons through you, and I thank God daily for you and the entire Norris family for standing behind me (Momma Norris, I still owe you coffee – lol)! You're indeed my ace on the scene and behind the scene, sowing and growing this amazing dream team. You're right, as I grow, you grow for sho! You're me and munchkin's common and my Gemini twin—we simply can't imagine the journey without you!

To Angela Jackson: You're the best friend, armor bearer, and virtual Assistant in the world! I love you to pieces. It's time to come out of ALL-BANY!

(Angela Jackson)

To Belle Nartey: Thank God for your spirit and your ability to read me and cover me. You are the best-kept jewel in my arsenal. Thank you!

To Rodney & Gena Lamb: My sister and brother! Thank you for the TRUTH and your truth! Thank you for the righteousness and for seeing something in me.

Thank you for bringing me into the world of taxation and for giving me an opportunity to seize #truthinduced and #yourtaxgirl for life!

To Janice aka J9, my one-woman glam squad: "She" loves you. It's just the beginning! To Robin D. Groover, my fierce natural hair glam diva: You are the reason why my

groove came back. I didn't see it then in 2006, but I surely get it now! The "She Box" and Groove Global = Billions!

To Seven and the Seventh Wonder crew: Thank you for helping me create this amazing brand and for the years to come!

To Anthony Grant: Thanks for in boxing me and for that $349.95 to get started!

To Jil Greene, Queen: Thank you for letting me serve you in our season. I was saddened to see you go, but because of it, I was forced to grow! I love you lady, and I'm so glad to have you back in my life!

To Ingrid: Thank you for praying for me when I couldn't pray for myself. I see you and thank you ladybug!

To my Bishop Joseph E. Sampson, PhD: Thank you for birthing me in my walk. You will never begin to know what you've done in my life.

To "Big L" from the home of the Jazz festival, Crawfish and Jambalaya: Thank you for all you've done!

To my amazing Pastor Anthony & His First Lady, Byrdzetta "Birdie" Knotts: Thank you for becoming my spiritual covering in this season—no photos of me sleeping in that orange chair, please.

To my beloved partner, Bishop Wayne Malcolm: Thank you for loving me unconditionally and embracing all of me and for bringing "She Speaks" to print.

To Mark Sterling: Thank you for helping realize that I am just one who can impact many!

(Anthony Knotts, Chinaza, Mark Sterling & Bishop Wayne Malcolm)

To Mena, my Dredhead sister in Oakland: Thank you for blessing me with "Chinaza," as God does indeed answer prayers.

To my children, Indira and LJ: Thank you for choosing me as mom and for being patient with mommy all the times she couldn't play or pay because she was out on the grind "making a provision" and doing what God would have her to do.

(Chinaza Duson and Indira Dutchin {Daughter}, May 2015)

(Langston Jr. {L.J.}, age 8, and Indira, age 9)

To Momma Banks: You truly are an angel. It does indeed take a village, and I thank you for providing me with one.

To Jacoree Prothro: Thank you for keeping me fitted when the money was funny and for introducing me to my anthem, "I'm Still Here" by Dorinda Clark Cole!

To my ace in the hole, the love of my life, and my sister from another mister, "Lyric," a.k.a. Ms. Kina, my right hand: Thank you for believing in me, keeping me ground, putting me in check, and for the turkey neck dinners during the rough times. Girl, it won't be long now!

To Christopher Lewis: Thank you for designing the Born Free tattoo on my shoulder and for your amazing friendship! Blessings to you and your family!

To George Tisdale, my brother from another mother: I can never ever forget about you, I've just been underground, making it happen and hoping you're proud. Thank you, Kim, for lending me your hubby in an amazing season!

To Devon Fairley: Thank you for helping me bring the verse-by-verse to this project!

To my first editor, Renee, Sista Girl, Devil Dogg, Semper Fi: I've never met you in person, but I love you because you believe in me enough to cover me during the initial draft of this project. I know God's has a special blessing in place for you, simply because you saw the vision and jumped on board to make it plain!

To Bertha: Girl, thank you for the prophetic word during our poetic sessions.

To the "Voices" team: A double shout out!

To my screenwriter who wrote the movie to support this project: There's only one way to go from here!

To anyone else I left out: I've not forgotten, just as God hasn't!

To all my supports and observers: Thank you!!! It is my prayer that God will discern into you your purpose, heal your land, loose you in destiny, and bless you in all modes of prosperity!

> *"Oh, that you would bless me indeed*
> *and enlarge my territory that you would be with*
> *me and that you would keep me from evil,*
> *that I may not cause pain."*
> *"Prayer of Jabez," I Chronicles, 4:10.*

In memory of my amazing leader who told me to, "Occupy until he comes!—Pastor Larry Townsend. I will wave the banner in your honor! I love you, Lady Mildred Townsend!

(Pastor Larry Townsend, Chinaza Duson, Lady Mildred Townsend)

(Chinaza Duson, Sundance Festival)

She shall speak for the voiceless –
until the voiceless can speak for themselves!
www.shespeaksworldwide.com
Chinaza@shespeaksworldwide.com
(404) 464.6733 – Media Relations

She Speaks